CHILDTIMES

Childtimes

A THREE-GENERATION MEMOIR

· BY ·

Eloise Greenfield

· AND ·

Lessie Jones Little

With material by Pattie Ridley Jones

DRAWINGS BY JERRY PINKNEY

AND PHOTOGRAPHS FROM THE AUTHORS' FAMILY ALBUMS

HarperTrophy

A Division of HarperCollins*Publishers*

Childtimes: A Three-Generation Memoir
Copyright © 1979 by Eloise Greenfield and Lessie Jones Little
Copyright © 1971 by Pattie Ridley Jones
All rights reserved. No part of this book may be used or reproduced in any manner
whatsoever without written permission except in the case of brief quotations
embodied in critical articles and reviews. Printed in the United States of America.
For information address HarperCollins Children's Books, a division of
HarperCollins Publishers, 1350 Avenue of the Americas, New York, NY 10019.

Library of Congress Cataloging-in-Publication Data
Greenfield, Eloise.
  Childtimes: a three-generation memoir
  Summary: Childhood memoirs of three black women—grandmother, mother,
and daughter—who grew up between the 1880's and 1950's.
  ISBN 0-06-446134-3 (pbk.)
  1. Jones, Pattie Ridley—Juvenile literature.   2. Little, Lessie Jones—Juvenile
literature.   3. Greenfield, Eloise—Juvenile literature.   4. Parmele, N.C.—
Biography—Juvenile literature.   5. Washington, D.C.—Biography—Juvenile
literature.   6. Afro-American children—Biography—Juvenile literature.
[1. Jones, Pattie Ridley.   2. Little, Lessie Jones.   3. Greenfield, Eloise.   4. Afro-
Americans—Biography.   I. Little, Lessie Jones, joint author.   II. Jones, Pattie
Ridley.   III. Pinkney, Jerry.   IV. Title.
F264.P37G73   1979   77-26581
920'.0092'96073
[920]

Designed by Trish Parcell
First Harper Trophy edition, 1993

Visit us on the World Wide Web!
www.harperchildrens.com

Acknowledgments
For their generous assistance in locating photographs, furnishing information, and
refreshing our memories, we are deeply grateful to Mr. Weston W. Little, Sr., Mrs.
Mary Harding, Mrs. Mattie Ridley, Mr. Robert J. Greenfield, Mrs. Mabel Mitchell,
Mrs. Roland Epperson, Mrs. Lillie Draper Taylor, Mr. Gerald Little, Mr. Weston
W. Little, Jr., Ms. Dorothy Greenfield, Mr. David L. Jones, Mrs. Carolyn Spencer,
Mrs. Vivian Savage, Mrs. Myrtle Jones, Mrs. Rosalie Andrews, Mr. John Andrews,
Mrs. Rosa Purvis, Mr. William Harriston, Jr., Mrs. Vera Mosley, and Mr. James Pitt.

Some of the material in Pattie Ridley Jones' section of this memoir appeared
previously in a booklet entitled *Looking Back*, published privately by the family of
Mrs. Jones in 1971.

Get on board, little children
Get on board, little children
Get on board, little children
There's room for many a more.
　　　　—BLACK SPIRITUAL

Contents

Landscape / *viii*   *Family Tree* / *x*   *Procession* / *xi*

PART I

Pattie Frances Ridley Jones · 1

PART II

Lessie Blanche Jones Little · 49

PART III

Eloise Glynn Little Greenfield · 119

Epilogue / 177

Landscape

❦

People are a part of their time. They are affected, during the time that they live, by the things that happen in their world. Big things and small things. A war, an invention such as radio or television, a birthday party, a kiss. All of these experiences help to shape people, and they, in turn, help to shape the present and the future. If we could know more about our ancestors, about the experiences they had when they were children, and after they had grown up, too, we would then know much more about what has shaped us and our world.

This book is about three children and their times, the times in which they grew up. It's about how those times were similar and how they were different.

This book is about family. Kinsfolk touching across the centuries, walking with one hand clasping the hands of those who have gone before, the other hand reaching back for those who will come after.

This book, most of all, is about black people struggling, not just to stay alive, but to live, to give of their talents, whether to many or few. Through all of their pain and grief, and even their mistakes, black people have kept on going, had some good times, given a lot of love to one another, and never stopped trying to help their children get on board the freedom train.

There's a lot of crying in this book, and there's dying, too, but there's also new life and laughter. It's all part of living.

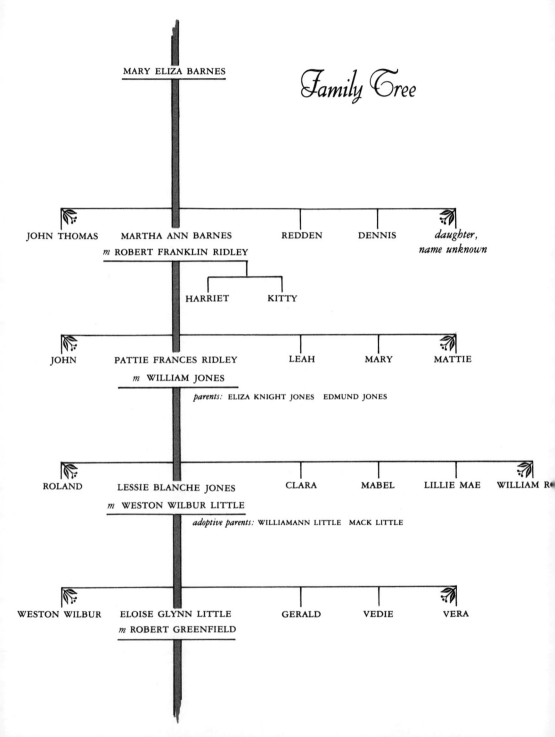

MARY ELIZA BARNES

Family Tree

JOHN THOMAS   MARTHA ANN BARNES   REDDEN   DENNIS   *daughter,*
name unknown
m ROBERT FRANKLIN RIDLEY

HARRIET   KITTY

JOHN   PATTIE FRANCES RIDLEY   LEAH   MARY   MATTIE
m WILLIAM JONES

parents: ELIZA KNIGHT JONES   EDMUND JONES

ROLAND   LESSIE BLANCHE JONES   CLARA   MABEL   LILLIE MAE   WILLIAM R●
m WESTON WILBUR LITTLE

adoptive parents: WILLIAMANN LITTLE   MACK LITTLE

WESTON WILBUR   ELOISE GLYNN LITTLE   GERALD   VEDIE   VERA
m ROBERT GREENFIELD

Procession

❦

We came, one behind the other, to our childtimes—grandmother, mother, daughter—just three marchers in a procession that stretches long and wide. Stretches across the ocean to the continent of Africa, back to great-grandmothers and great-grandfathers and great-greats and great-great-greats, and on and on, all the way back to the beginning of human life on earth. Stretches outward to sisters and brothers and aunts and uncles and nephews and nieces and cousins. A long, wide, family procession with thousands of marchers. We are just three.

Pattie Frances Ridley Jones

BORN IN BERTIE COUNTY, NORTH CAROLINA,

December 15, 1884

LANDSCAPE

🌷

THE 1880's *were years of movement in the United States. Miles and miles of railroad tracks were being laid across the country. Large numbers of people were moving west, pushing Native Americans from their homes, to form new states—North Dakota, South Dakota, and others—to add to the nation. Most black people, however, remained in the South, and these were disappointing years for them.*

During slavery, black people had looked forward to a time when they would be free. Many of them had risked their lives to take part in the struggle to end slavery, refusing to work, forming groups to fight the slaveowners, escaping to the North to tell what it was like to be enslaved. Some, the ex-slave woman, Sojourner Truth, among them, had demanded both an end to slavery and equal rights for blacks and women. And, during the Civil War, almost two hundred thousand black people had joined the northern army and fought against the South. When slavery was finally outlawed, they were overjoyed. But the kind of freedom they had expected did not come.

White farmers were angry because they now had to pay black workers. They kept the pay low, and in some states, blacks who didn't have jobs could be forced to work without receiving wages. In many areas, black schools and homes were burned, and people were dragged from their homes and murdered, by a group called the Ku Klux Klan. It was hard to stay alive, hard to get jobs, hard to get an education.

This was the world into which Pattie Ridley was born.

PATTIE FRANCES RIDLEY JONES

❦

It's been a good long time since my childtime. Yours is now, you're living your childtime right this minute, but I've got to go way, way back to remember mine.

Memory is a funny thing. You never know how it's going to act. A lot of things that I saw and heard, and heard about, when I was a girl, I can't call to mind at all now. My memory just hop-skips right over them. Some other things, I can almost remember, but when I try to catch hold of them, they get mixed up with something else, or disappear. But then, there are the things that keep coming back, keep coming back just as plain, just as clear. . . .

About My Mother's Mother

Mary Eliza Barnes would one day be my grandmama, but when she was young, she was held a slave in Bertie County, a large farming area in North Carolina. She told my mama about it when Mama was a little girl, and Mama told me.

I don't know Grandmama's real last name. She wasn't allowed to use it. Slaves had to go by the name that the white family had, the family that the law said owned them, and Grandmama was held by the Barnes family. They made her work out in the fields all day, every day. Sick or well, good weather or bad, she had to work. And after slavery was over, she kept on working in those same fields for a little bit of pay and a place to live. She didn't know any other way to make a living, and she stayed there for a good while.

Some of Grandmama's children were born on that farm. One of them was named Martha Ann.

The Dumb Supper

When Martha Ann Barnes was a little girl, some new neighbors moved to Bertie County. They were the Ridleys from over in Oxford, North Carolina. Robert Franklin Ridley and his wife, Maria, and their two daughters, Harriet and Kitty.

Those two little girls and Martha got to be the best of friends, and they played together every chance they got. Martha couldn't play as much as she wanted to because she wasn't free. Slavery was over and she wasn't a slave, but she wasn't free, either. She had to be a maid for the Barnes family. But every minute she could, she spent at the Ridleys'. She even got to calling Mr. and Mrs. Ridley Uncle Bob and Aunt Maria.

One day, the girls decided to play a game called "dumb supper." It was a game to see who you would marry. Harriet and Kitty and Martha all sat around the dinner table with their plates turned down, and nobody was talking. They weren't supposed to talk, and the kitchen window had been raised so that, by some kind of magic, a man would come through the window and turn up the plate of the girl he would marry.

Uncle Bob was sitting there watching them, and they were all quiet and waiting, waiting for something to happen, when all of a sudden a strong wind came up. And while that wind was blowing, it thundered the loudest thunder they had ever heard, and a big dog that nobody had ever seen before jumped through the window. Well, Uncle Bob stood up and told them to cut out that dumb supper! And that was the end of that.

Mister Ridley

When Martha was fifteen years old, after Aunt Maria had been dead for some years, she and Uncle Bob fell in love and wanted to get married. Martha's mother was good

and mad with her for wanting to marry a man old enough
to be her father. But things were different in those days.
Back then, most girls thought the only thing they could
do when they grew up was get married and take care of
the house, and raise a family. So Martha kept on
worrying her mother about it.

After a while, her mother told her to go ahead. Go
ahead and get married, if that was what she wanted to do.
So Martha Ann Barnes and Robert Franklin Ridley got
married, but she got so much teasing from the people
around there for calling her husband Uncle Bob that she
didn't want to call him that any more. She started calling
him Mister Ridley. Only she said it fast, like one
word—Mistridley. And she called him that as long as he
lived.

Well, they were my mama and papa, and they had five
children. John, then me, then Leah, Mary, and Mattie.
We never did see our half sisters, Harriet and Kitty.
They had stayed with Mama and Papa for a time, but
Harriet was taken sick with TB and died, and Kitty went

back to Oxford and got married. We did see Kitty's picture, though. Mama kept it put away in her trunk, and we children called the picture Sis Kitty.

We loved Harriet and Kitty, even if we didn't really know them. We heard a lot about them from Mama and Papa, all about them being Mama's best friends and about the dumb supper. And we never did find out what happened to that big dog, because every time they got to the part about Papa jumping up and saying, "Stop this dumb supper!" we'd fall all over the place, just laughing.

Parmele, North Carolina

Towns build up around work, you know. People go and live where they can find jobs. And that's how Parmele got started.

At first, it was just a junction, a place where two railroads crossed. Two Atlantic Coast Line railroads, one running between Rocky Mount and Plymouth, and one running between Kinston and Weldon. Didn't too many people live around there then, and those that did were pretty much spread out.

Well, around 1888, a Yankee named Mr. Parmele came down from New York and looked the place over, and he saw all those big trees and decided to start a lumber company. Everybody knew what that meant. There were going to be jobs! People came from everywhere to get work. I was right little at that time, too little to know what was going on, but everybody says it was something to see how fast that town grew. All those people moving in and houses going up. They named the town after the man who made the jobs, and they called it *Pomma-lee.*

The lumber company hired a whole lot of people. They hired workers to lay track for those little railroads they call tram roads that they were going to run back and forth between the town and the woods. They hired lumberjacks to chop the trees down and cut them up into logs, and load them on the tram cars. They hired men to build the mill and put the machinery in, and millworkers to run the machines that would cut the logs into different sizes and dry them and make them nice and smooth.

That wood was some kind of pretty when it was finished, too. Some of it was sold in our town to people who had the money to buy ceilings for their houses, but most of it was shipped to other places. Mr. Parmele made a whole lot of money. Not too many people liked him, not too many white people, anyway. Even though he was white, too, he was from the North, he was a Yankee, and they hadn't forgotten about the Civil War. He made a whole lot of money, though. He had so many people working for him that he had this special store built just for them, a commissary, where they could buy what they needed—groceries, and medicine, and shoes, and yard goods, just about anything they needed.

He had houses built, too, two-story houses. Right close to the commissary, they built houses for the white workers and their families, and they painted them white.

And out a ways from there, he had some more houses built, ten of them, but he didn't have those painted. They were for the black workers, and twenty families had to live in those ten houses. That was the part of Parmele they called Sugar Hill.

Well, after a good many years—about eighteen, I guess—the mill had to be closed down. Just about all of those great big trees were gone. Mr. Parmele moved his lumber mill away, to South Carolina if I remember right, and that didn't leave too many jobs in our town. A lot of people left, a lot of people. They moved to other places, looking for work.

Papa's Jobs

We were living in a little place called Robersonville, about three miles from Parmele, when Papa heard about the mill going up. He had been down sick with a bad case of rheumatism around that time, and Mama and all of us had been real worried about him, but he was better by then and walking on crutches. So early one morning he took the train to go see about getting a job.

They hired Papa, and that's when we moved to Parmele. Papa got seventy-five cents a day for feeding the horses that pulled the wagonloads of machines—saws and things—from the train station to the mill. And when all the machinery was in, he got the job of cooking at the clubhouse where the company's officers lived, and cleaning up their bedrooms and the dining room. The clubhouse was different from most all the houses around Parmele. It had radiators, and pipes running from the mill, for steam heat in the wintertime. There was even a bathtub, it was in the dining room, and pipes for hot and cold running water, and hardly anybody had that in their houses.

Papa worked at the clubhouse until the mill closed down, and then he stayed on as the night watchman.

16

After all the machines had been taken out and shipped away, Papa spent his nights there, watching those empty buildings.

Mr. John Draper

Everybody around Parmele knew Mr. John Draper, and everybody liked him, too. He waited on people in the commissary, and he was just as nice as he could be. People would come in with their wooden baskets over their arms, and Mr. John Draper would get them what they wanted and pack it in the baskets so nice and neat.

He sold things door to door, too. All kinds of sweet things like cakes and doughnuts. He had a basket just full of good things, but he didn't carry it over his arm. He carried it on his head. Didn't even have to hold it. Walked right along steady with it the way

17

his ancestors had done in Africa. I used to think to my-self, It's going to spill, it's going to spill, and all those goodies are going to be lying out in the road. But it never did.

One time, Mr. John Draper gave a big festival. That was after I got to be a pretty big girl. He hadn't gotten married yet at that time, and he was living by himself upstairs over an empty store building. Well, he set up tables on the first floor and put refreshments on all the tables, and he asked Mr. Stanley Barnhill to come from Bethel to sing.

People from all over came to that festival. They came from neighboring towns and from all out in the country, and everywhere. Mr. Stanley Barnhill sang, "Traveling, I've Got on My Traveling Shoes," and I got in line with my fella like all the other young girls, and we marched. We couldn't dance, dancing was a sin. But we marched, I'm telling you! We marched around and around that room until we got too tired to take another step. Then we

went up to the tables, and our fellas treated us to punch
and little cakes.

We had the best old time, and I kept thinking it sure
was nice of Mr. John Draper to do this for us.

Our House

Papa built our house. It was shaped like a capital L lying
down on its side. Well no, to tell you the truth, it was
more like three L's sandwiched together—the back
porch, and the front porch, and the house in the middle.
It was made of wood mostly, but right at the corner of
the front bedroom, there was a big brick chimney that
started on the ground and went way up taller than the
house.

We had three rooms and a hall and a kitchen. One of
the front rooms was Mama and Papa's, and the other one

THIS PAGE: *Martha Ann Barnes Ridley and grandson Robert Franklin Ridley (named for his grandfather), 1921.* OPPOSITE PAGE, clockwise from top left: *Eliza Knight Jones, early 1930's; H. Ferdinand Highsmith, c. 1900; John Draper, c. 1911; William and Pattie Ridley Jones, Parmele, 1925.*

was my brother John's. We girls had the back room. I can remember that Papa painted one of the rooms blue, a soft kind of blue, but I can't for the life of me remember which room it was.

The kitchen was the place where Mama and Papa liked to sit in the evening after Papa got off from work. I remember one time Papa came home with a piece of wood for my youngest sister, Mattie. It was a short plank from the mill. Mattie was real little then, and he always brought her something, a stick of candy or some little something, and this time he brought her this plank. Well, Mattie was so happy. When Mama and Papa sat in the kitchen that night, she rested the ends of the plank on the rounds of their chairs and then sat on it, and she just sat there looking back and forth from one to the other while they talked.

I liked to be inside the house most of the time doing quiet kinds of things. Reading, and learning poems. I liked to play Sunday School with my little sisters when I could keep them still long enough. They'd let me teach them Bible lessons for a little while, but not for long. First thing I'd know, they'd dash for the door and there they'd be for the rest of the day, Mary, Mattie, and Leah, running and playing in the yard.

We had a nice big backyard with all kinds of flowers that Mama had planted, just about every kind of flower you can think of, and then a fence that went all the way around the house. Outside the fence there was a ditch for the water to drain into when it rained. And then our garden, a big vegetable garden with collards and cucumbers and sweet potatoes and butter beans, all kinds of things.

When Mary and Leah got to be pretty big girls, they planted four trees, elm trees, in the front yard. After a while, Mama cut two of them down, but the other two grew up so full and pretty. Our house is gone now, it's been gone right many years, but one of those trees is standing there yet.

Water

We didn't have running water. At first we had a well out in the backyard, until it started caving in and Papa had to get rid of it. He filled it in with dirt. Then every time we wanted water for bathing or drinking or washing clothes, we had to go get water from a neighbor's pump. We got so tired of carrying those buckets of water, and we were some kind of glad when Papa finally put a pump on our back porch.

Mattie's Ride

We had a horse named George, and one day when Papa was going to Robersonville or somewhere, on business, he hitched George to the buggy and went back in the house to get something. Well, my little sister Mattie got in the buggy—she and Lillian, her friend Lottie Belle's sister—and they picked up the reins and George started off, started right off walking down the road. Such screaming and yelling you never heard. And poor Papa, he had to run down there and catch them.

More About My Mother's Mother

I had never laid eyes on Grandmama, to remember, when Mama and Papa said we could go on a trip to visit her. They said we were big enough to go by ourselves, all except Mattie, she was too little. My brother was the biggest, he was about twelve then, and he was put in charge of the rest of us.

Grandmama lived on a big farm in a place called Sea Landing, and we would have to take a train and a boat to get there. Mama packed our clothes and she and Papa took us to the train station. Mama kept saying don't forget to do this, and don't forget to do that, and I was saying, "Yes ma'am, yes ma'am," but I was in a hurry for that train to get moving. Well, it finally did, and we were on our way.

We got off the train in Williamston and got in a hack. That's what they used to call cabs, only back then a cab wasn't a car, there weren't any cars on the streets. The hack was a horse and carriage, and we climbed up in it and told the driver to take us to Mrs. Rhodes' house. And that's where we spent the night.

Real early the next morning, about five o'clock, Mrs. Rhodes took us down to the dock, and there was the boat, the *Haven Belle*. It was a funny-looking little thing, kind of like a wooden house, with a narrow walkway going all the way around and windows all around, too. We went inside and sat down on some long benches, and we sat there all the way, looking out the window at the water.

When we got to Sea Landing, Mama's brother, Uncle Redden, met us and took us to Grandmama's, and she was so happy to see us. She just hugged us and kissed us, and the whole time we were there, she was cooking us good things to eat and doing everything to let us have a good time. Every morning after breakfast, she would tell us to go out to the plum trees and eat all we wanted. She had a whole lot of plum trees, and those leaves were so thick and close together that just a few tiny dots of sunlight could get through. We'd sit on the grass under the trees and eat until our stomachs almost popped.

One day Grandmama made us some molasses pudding, and we had always loved molasses pudding. Dark brown and kind of moist, like gingerbread. We held out our plates while Grandmama cut a big piece for each one of us. We said, "Thank you, ma'am," and went out under the trees to eat it. But when we tasted it, it wasn't like the kind Mama made. It wasn't made with flour, it was made with cornmeal. Well, I tell you, it was some kind of bad-tasting, but we didn't want to hurt Grandmama's feelings, so we went way out away from the house and threw that molasses pudding as far as we could. And when Grandmama asked us if we liked it, we said, "Yes, ma'am."

After a while, our visit was over, and we took the *Haven Belle* back to Williamston and the train back to the Parmele station. Mama and Papa were waiting for us, and we all talked at the same time, telling about what a good time we had.

When Grandmama got old, Uncle Redden wanted her to come live with him, but she didn't want to live with any of her children. She wanted to live by herself. So Uncle Redden built a house for her in his yard, and every morning he would send one of his boys to look in on her to be sure she was all right. One morning, when the boy got there, Grandmama had died.

We were so sad when we got the news. Mama packed some of her clothes and took the train to go to the funeral. But not many people had telephones back then, and the news had come late. By the time Mama got to the cemetery, they were lowering the casket into the grave, and they had to bring it back up so Mama could get one last look at her mother. Then Uncle Redden took sick, he took sick right there at the burial, and he didn't live but a few more days. It was a real sad time for all of us.

Clothes

Mama made our dresses. Mattie's, Mary's, Leah's, and mine. Papa used to buy a whole bolt of cloth, and all of us would have a dress made out of that same material. We thought we were really something in those dresses. Long-sleeved dresses with yokes. The bottom part was gathered on the yoke and hung down loose to just below the knee. We wore sailor hats with streamers and bows, and high-topped shoes and heavy ribbed stockings up to the knee. We'd put these wide rubber bands, about an inch wide, around the tops of our stockings to keep them from falling down.

Mama made us take good care of our clothes, too. We'd better not get them messed up. She'd say, "Your papa worked hard to get these clothes." She wouldn't even whip us in our dresses when we did something wrong. She made us take them off first. And Mama could really whip! If any grown-up told her that we'd been bad, we knew we were going to get it.

Mama would march right out to those little black gum bushes growing in our yard, and she'd cut off a skinny branch and strip all the leaves off. And then she'd bring that switch back and she'd say, "Come on, young lady." We'd better not take too long getting there, either. But before she whipped us, she'd say, "Take that dress off. I ain't going to whip out these clothes your papa bought."

Mama could whip, I'm telling you. She could get so mad. But she didn't ever get mad enough to forget about those clothes.

Chores

We had right much work to do. In the house and out in the garden, too. We planted and weeded, and dug up sweet potatoes, and picked butter beans. Papa let us sell the beans and keep the money for ourselves.

We had to keep the yards clean, too, front and back. Most people didn't have grass in their yards. They had dirt yards, and we would sweep our yards every day, get up all the loose dirt, and leave them brushed clean, with the brush strokes the yard broom made looking almost like a design.

My sister Mary and I did the cooking. Some weeks she cooked and some weeks I cooked. We had one of those big iron stoves that you put coal in to make a fire, and that stove would get so hot, not just on the cooking eyes, but all over. When we did the ironing, we'd set the irons on the stove to heat them up. Our irons were heavy, they were made of real iron, even the handles, and we had to use a thick piece of cloth to hold them. We had four or five irons, and we'd iron with one until it got too cool and then we'd pick up another one, and keep on like that until we got the ironing done.

We had feather beds. The mattresses were stuffed with chicken feathers, and we had to turn them over nearly every day, and we couldn't miss a day shaking them up and smoothing out all the lumps. They had to be exactly right, just as smooth and neat, or Mama would make us do them all over again.

We didn't pull our bedspreads all the way up over the pillows the way a lot of people do nowadays. We had pillow shams that Mama had made, white cotton material that she cut in the shape of the pillow and embroidered. Sometimes she put lace around the edges, and she kept them starched so stiff and ironed so pretty. We would tack the top of the sham on to the head of the bedstead with thumbtacks, and after we finished making up the rest of the bed, we'd stand the pillows up and let the shams hang down in front of them. It was a pretty sight. Then at night when we went to bed we'd fold the shams back over the head of the bedstead so they wouldn't get wrinkled.

When you finished making up a bed, you knew better than to sit on it. Wherever you sat, those chicken feathers would mash flat and they'd stay mashed, and then you'd have to take everything off and start all over, shaking and patting to get it right again. We wouldn't ever sit on the bed. We already had enough chores to do, we sure didn't want to do anything twice.

School

The school we went to was a one-room schoolhouse, a little square building with a big old potbellied stove inside. In the winter, the boys used to take turns going to school early in the morning to start the fire in the stove. That fire would be just blazing when the rest of us got there, and the room would be so warm.

Our seats were long benches, and we didn't have desks. We wrote on slates in our laps with a little piece of chalk. Mr. Highsmith—that was our teacher—he used to walk up and down between the benches, smiling, while we studied our books. Spelling books, reading books, arithmetic books. We had to study, study, study. We'd be some kind of glad when twelve o'clock came and we could go out for recess.

Most of the time we played in the schoolyard, but sometimes when the weather was nice and warm, we'd walk a ways from the school to a road where there were all these mulberry trees with ripe mulberries just waiting to be picked. We'd find some lightwood knots, those little pieces of pine wood you see lying in the woods sometimes, and we'd throw them up at the branches to knock the berries down. We had the best old time eating and getting our faces and hands all purple and sticky.

When recess was over, Mr. Highsmith would ring this little bell like the one Mama rang for us to come in to dinner. But if we were right in the schoolyard, he wouldn't ring the bell. He'd come to the schoolhouse door and call, "Books! Books!" He meant it was time for us to get back to those books and study some more.

John and the Snake

A terrible thing happened to my brother John in the schoolyard one day. He and his friends were running and playing in the deep grass, and John said to his friends, "I bet you can't throw me down!" Well, they jumped on him and threw him down, and they were holding him down there, and all of a sudden he felt this sharp pain in his wrist.

John said, "Get off me! Somebody stuck me with a pin!"

They said, "No we didn't," but John felt it again. Then one of the boys saw this old snake wriggling through the grass, trying to get away. It was one of those poisonous snakes, too, a moccasin, and the boys ran after it and killed it with some sticks. Then they rushed John into school to tell Mr. Highsmith.

Mr. Highsmith took his handkerchief and tied it tight around John's arm, right up above his elbow, so the poison wouldn't go to his heart, and he chewed some tobacco and laid it to John's wrist. Then John and some of his friends went to the mill to get Papa.

Papa was so worried. He did everything he could think of to do. First he put some alcohol on it, then somebody told him to cut open a black chicken and put that to it, so he did that as soon as they got home. Then he went out in the country and got the snake doctor.

That snake doctor knew what he was doing all right. He put this special kind of tea on the stove to brew, and he sent my sister Mary to the store to get three plugs of tobacco to cut up in it, and as soon as it was ready, he gave a cup of it to John. Well, that tea didn't stay in his stomach a hot minute. It came right back up, and it was as yellow as the yellow of an egg.

Mama turned her head away, and she said, "Oh mister, you ain't doing my child a bit of good," but the doctor gave John another cup and the same thing happened. We waited for the third cup to come back up, too, but it didn't, so the doctor said all the poison was out of John's body.

I looked at my brother lying in that bed and I just knew he was going to die. He looked so weak and sick, and his hand had swelled up so, it looked like his fingers were about to split open. We sat up with him all night, all of us, his friends, too. The room was full of schoolchildren trying to stay awake and watch John, and in the morning he was better. That doctor had sure known what he was doing.

John stayed in bed for about a week, and he had to sit

around the house for two or three more weeks; then he was well enough to go back to school. But you could still see the print of those two holes on his wrist where the snake had punched its fangs in. All the children wanted to get a look at them, and John didn't mind a bit showing them off.

Getting Baptized

When we moved to Parmele, right after Papa got his job feeding horses at the lumber mill, there wasn't a single place of worship in the town. So Mama used to go back to Robersonville to the Baptist church there, once a month, Saturday and Sunday. But finally Mama and Papa got some people together to start holding church meetings in a vacant house.

At first they called the church the Parmele Missionary

Baptist Church. Then, they raised enough money to buy land and build their own building, and it was named Ridley's Chapel in honor of Mama and Papa. Later on, they changed it to Olive Branch Baptist Church, and that church is still there, not the same building but the one they put up after the old one burned down.

I was baptized at Olive Branch, baptized in deep water, when I was twelve years old. John and I, and a lot of other people. The day before the baptism, one of the deacons went down to the creek that was way out from the church, and he took this long pole with him to poke around in the water and see how deep it was, and to find any holes that might be dangerous. Then he left the pole standing in the water and that was as far out as anybody was supposed to go.

The next morning Mama and Papa took us to church, and everybody who was getting baptized wrapped a white cloth around their heads, and all the women and girls put on white gowns. We got in line and walked to the creek with the whole congregation going along with us. And everybody was just singing. *"Take me to the wa-a-ter, take me to the wa-a-ter, take me to the wa-a-ter, to be bap-tized."* And the deacon was taking people, one by one, down into the water so Reverend Riddick could baptize them and send them back up on the bank.

When it came my turn, I stepped into the water and it was cold, and my heart was just pounding, but I went on out to Reverend Riddick. He took my left hand and put it on my chest, and he put my right hand on top of my left hand. Then he leaned me backwards toward the water, all the while talking, saying, "I baptize you in the name of the Father and the Son and the Holy Ghost." Then he dipped my head down under the water real fast and stood me right straight up again. He said, "Amen," and he put his hand on my forehead and wiped down my face kind of hard and fast so I wouldn't breathe in any water, and it was all over.

I was baptized.

Candy

We used to have parties we called candy crackings. I remember the very first one Papa had for us. He and Mr. Slade Barnhill bought a lot of hard candy and a new tin tub. They cracked the candy up into small pieces and put it in little bags and put the bags in the tub. Then they hung up this sheet for a curtain and set the tub behind it, and after we had played post office and pin the tail on the donkey, we played fishing. The fishing pole was a reed with a string tied to it. We'd stick the fishing pole behind the curtain and somebody back there, Papa or Mr. Slade, would tie a bag of candy to it, and we'd pull it back. We had right much fun doing that, pretending we had caught a bag of candy.

Sometimes we had candy pullings. We'd put sugar and a little vinegar in a brass kettle and set it on the stove, and as soon as the sugar got hot, the vinegar would dissolve it. Then we cooked it until it hardened some, just a little, not too much, and we'd pour it in a platter that had been greased with butter. When the candy cooled enough, two of us would put butter on our hands and we'd pick up the candy, one of us at one end and one at the other, and we'd pull it, kind of easy like. When we started pulling, it would be brown, but after we had stretched it enough, it looked right silvery. Then we'd lay it all around on the platter and break it into sticks. It used to look so pretty, I almost didn't want to eat it.

The Jones Family

When I was about fourteen, a Mr. and Mrs. Jones moved to Parmele. Edmund and Eliza Knight Jones and their ten children. There were three sons and seven daughters. The Jones family bought two acres of land not far from our house, and they had a one-and-a-half-story house built on it. Two large rooms and a hall were on the first floor, and the second floor was an attic with a real low ceiling. It was so low, a grown person couldn't stand up in it, so it was used for the boys to sleep in.

Mrs. Jones loved to read. She used to teach school sometimes, and she loved books. She wanted all of her children to be able to read, so she taught the big ones and the big ones taught the little ones. Mrs. Jones used to sell chicken eggs for ten cents a dozen to buy books for her children. A book cost fifteen cents, and that was a lot of money back then.

One day there was a big windstorm in Parmele, and I mean that was some storm! It blew the Jones' house over. Nobody got hurt, but Mrs. Jones and two of her daughters had to go to work to save money for a new house. They went to Greenville and worked in the tobacco factory, pulling the stems off the tobacco leaves, until they had enough money. The family did most all the work on the new house themselves. They couldn't afford to buy nails, and their fingers bled from pulling the nails out of the old house to use again.

My favorite person in the Jones family was William, the oldest one of their children. When I got old enough to have a fella, William was my fella. We went to church together and sang in the choir together. And Sunday evenings, Mama would let us go for a walk down to the train station to watch the trains come in, and see the people passing through town. I was old enough to wear long dresses by then and I would get all prettied up on a Sunday, and William would come and get me.

My little sisters, Mary and Leah, always wanted to go with us on our walks. They kept begging and begging until one day I told them to come on and go. So William and I were walking along kind of slow, and I was holding the back of my dress with one hand the way I'd seen the ladies do, lifting it up just the tiniest little bit. Well, I happened to look back and what were Mary and Leah doing but just switching along, holding the backs of their dresses, mocking me and giggling to beat the band!

Well, the Jones family were our neighbors for a good long while. My brother John married Roberta, one of the daughters, and on December 30, 1903, William Jones and I got married.

Leah's Wedding

When Leah was almost seventeen, she fell in love with Tom Moore, and they were married on a Wednesday night in September 1902. It was the first wedding ever held at Olive Branch Baptist Church. Leah wore a wreath on her head and white elbow gloves and a long dress trimmed in white silk ribbon. My sister was a beautiful bride.

There were six bridesmaids, and I can't remember now just who they were, but I was the maid of honor. Reverend Gilmore was our preacher at that time, and Tom stood up front with him, while we walked in slow, without any music or anything. First the bridesmaids, then me, then Leah on Papa's arm. It was a real quiet, pretty wedding.

After that, we went on back to our house for the reception, and the next morning the newlyweds left to go live in Portsmouth, Virginia. A lot of us went down to the train station to see them off. They were so happy and so much in love, and we couldn't keep from crying when the train pulled out.

Tom and Leah hardly had time to get settled in their new home. One morning, about three weeks after the wedding, Tom left for work and he never came back. He had a job on a train that carried logs from Portsmouth to some place in North Carolina, and that morning the train stopped at some little town, and Tom got off and was walking along the railroad tracks when the wire that fastened the logs to the train broke. It happened so fast that Tom didn't have a chance to get out of the way. All those logs rolled on top of him, and he was killed.

So . . . Leah came home a widow, all dressed in black, and she wasn't quite seventeen years old.

Well, William and I had the second wedding held at our church. After we were married, we stayed with his family for a while until he could finish the house he had started building, and then we went to live in our own three-room house. William and I had six children. Four of them lived to grow up. Four daughters. One of them was Lessie.

Lessie Blanche Jones Little

BORN IN PARMELE, NORTH CAROLINA,

October 1, 1906

LANDSCAPE

❧

THE TWENTIETH CENTURY was new, only six years old. Just three years had passed since the Wright brothers flew their famous airplane. Radio broadcasting had not yet begun. Telephones had been installed in only a small percentage of American homes. The automobile—that strange-looking machine that moved without having to be pulled—was seen so seldom that it was still scaring horses off the road. And fourteen more years would pass before women would win full voting rights.

Black people, in 1906, were continuing to look for ways to solve the problems they faced. Some started organizations that worked for an end to racism. One such organization was the Niagara Movement. The

*year that Lessie Jones was born, it issued to the nation
a list of demands for full rights for black people. One
of its demands was for the education of children. It said
that black children have a right to a real education, a
right to think, a right to know.*

❦

Sis Clara

Everybody says I can't remember when Clara died, that I was too little. But they're wrong. I was only three, but I remember.

I'm next to the oldest in my family. My sister Roland was first, then me, then Clara, Mabel, and Lillie Mae. William Robert Jones, Jr., was the youngest. He didn't live but eight hours. Clara was seventeen months old when she died.

I really don't remember her too well, I can't remember her face or anything like that, but I know I used to call her Sis Clara. And I can still see that little coffin sitting on two chairs in the bedroom, and my baby sister lying in it.

They put the coffin in a wagon that was hitched to two horses. I sat on somebody's lap and I didn't know where we were going, but we took the coffin somewhere and we didn't bring it back. We didn't bring Sis Clara back home. And Mama cried a lot.

Parmele

I used to hear Papa and Mama and their friends talking about the lumber mill that had been the center of life in Parmele before I was born, but there wasn't any mill when I was growing up. The only thing left of it was the sawdust from all the wood they had sawed there. The sawdust was about a foot thick on the land where the mill had been. I used to love to walk on it. It was spongy, and it made me feel like I was made of rubber. I'd take my shoes off and kind of bounce along on top of it. But that was all that was left of the mill.

My Parmele was a train town. The life of my town moved around the trains that came in and out all day long. About three hundred people lived in Parmele, most of them black. There were three black churches, a Baptist, a Methodist, and a Holiness, and one white church. Two black schools, one white. There wasn't even one doctor, and not many people would have had the money to pay one, if there had been. If somebody got down real bad sick, a member of the family would go by horse and buggy to a nearby town and bring the doctor back, or sometimes the doctor would ride on his own horse.

Most of the men and women in Parmele earned their living by farming. Some did other things like working at the tobacco factory in Robersonville, but most worked on the farms that were all around in the area, white people's farms usually. When I was a little girl, they earned fifty cents a day, a farm day, sunup to sundown, plus meals. After they got home, they had all their own work to do, cooking and cleaning, laundry, chopping wood for the woodstove, and shopping.

I used to love to go shopping with Mama. There was so much to see downtown. When people started getting cars, the only gasoline pump in town was down there. There were stores, four or five stores, where you could buy clothes, or yard goods, or groceries, or hardware, and the post office was in the corner of one store. Stokes' Cafe, where the white railroad workers ate, was on one side of the tracks, and Powell's Restaurant for the black workers was on the other side.

There was a little park, too, where we had picnics sometimes, and we had one policeman, and a jailhouse with two cells that were almost always empty, and one dance hall for the black people who thought it was all right to dance. The water tank and the coal chute where the trains got refills were downtown, and so was the train station.

Twice I lived in houses that the trains had to pass right by on their way to the station. I'd hear that whistle blow, and I'd run out on the porch just in time to see the train come twisting around the curve like a long black worm. I'd wave at the people sitting at the windows, and they'd wave back at me.

Trains weren't air-conditioned in those days, and when the weather was warm, the windows were always open. Black people had to sit in the front car so that whites wouldn't get dirty from the smoke and soot and cinders that blew in the windows from the engine.

I remember a train trip I took when I was small. I had on my pink organdy dress that Mama had made me, and I was so proud of the way I looked. But the whole time, I had to keep rubbing the cinders out of my eyes, and soot kept getting on my dress, and every time I tried to brush it off, it made a long, dirty streak. I was a mess by the time I got off the train. I was really dirty, my face and hands and my clothes, and my eyes were red and sore.

Parmele had trains coming in and going out all day long. Passenger trains and freight trains. There was always so much going on at the station that I wouldn't know what to watch. People were changing trains and going in and out of the cafe and the restaurant. They came from big cities like New York and Chicago and Boston, and they were all wearing the latest styles. Things were being unloaded, like furniture and trunks and plows and cases of fruit and crates of clucking chickens, or a puppy, or the body of somebody who had died and was being brought back home. And every year around the last two weeks in May, a special train would come through. It had two white flags flying on the locomotive, and it was carrying one hundred carloads of white potatoes that had been grown down near Pamlico Sound, where everybody said the soil was so rich they didn't even have to fertilize it.

The train station was a gathering place, too. A lot of people went there to relax after they had finished their work for the day. They'd come downtown to pick up their mail, or buy a newspaper, and then they'd just stand around laughing and talking to their friends. And on Sundays fellas and their girls would come all the way from other towns, just to spend the afternoon at the Parmele train station.

Hot Rolls

Every Sunday morning, Mama cooked a special breakfast. Beefsteak or pork chops, something like that. She and Papa had coffee or tea, and we had Postum. And rolls. Mama could make the best old rolls, they were some kind of good!

Before we could start eating, though, Papa had to pray. We would get down on our knees and rest our elbows on our chairs, and Papa would pray for a long time. Too long. I wasn't thinking about praying, I was thinking about eating.

Good old hot rolls with homemade butter and homemade preserves. As soon as I'd finish one I'd say, "Mama, thank you for another roll," and she'd put one on my plate. I'd keep on until Papa said, "Little duckie"— that's what he called us—"Little duckie," he'd say, "if you eat any more, you won't be able to get out of your chair." And that would be the end of that.

My Papa

Papa was a quiet man. He liked to read a lot, study his Bible and his Sunday School book and the newspaper. We took the *Raleigh News and Observer*. It came in every day on the train with the rest of the mail, and Papa would walk to the post office to get it. He walked with a slight limp because one leg was shorter than the other. The older he got, the shorter the leg seemed to get, and later in life he walked with a deep limp like his papa, but when I was growing up, it wasn't too bad.

Every winter morning Papa would get up early and build a fire in the heater in his and Mama's room, and he'd set a large pot of water on it so Mama could get bathed when she got up. Then he'd make a fire in the kitchen stove for cooking.

Those were the only two rooms with heat. The rest of the house was so cold. We hated so bad to get out of our warm beds when Mama called us, but finally we would jump up and snatch our clothes and run barefoot through the hall to Mama and Papa's room. Papa would say, "Come on in here, little duckies. Great day in the morning, I got a good fire going for you!"

When Papa got home in the evening, he'd get the fire in the bedroom going real good again, and after dinner we'd all go back to that warm room. Sometimes the heater was so hot, it glowed red. Mama and Papa would just sit and talk while we did our homework and enjoyed Papa's fire.

Papa sang bass in the church choir. He had a beautiful voice, such a beautiful voice. Everybody in his family could sing, and I think he could have been a professional singer if he had been born at a later time when there were more opportunities for black people. And he had the prettiest whistle I've ever heard. Everybody in Parmele knew Papa's whistle. Some notes he'd whistle in the regular way, but other notes he whistled in harmony— soprano, alto, tenor, one after the other real fast, almost like a tremble. Sometimes at night we'd hear it way, way down the road, and we'd be so glad because we knew it was Papa, coming home from work, whistling a hymn.

It was hard for Papa to find work. Not long after Sis Clara died, we moved to Mount Herman, a black section of Portsmouth, Virginia. Papa worked on the docks there, and even though he didn't make much money, the work was steady. But when we moved back to Parmele, it was hard for him to find any work at all.

Sometimes he worked on the railroad, cutting the grass that grew between the ties of the tracks. Sometimes he worked on white people's farms, but when they tried to treat him like a child, he told them that he was a man, and they fired him. For about two years he rented a small piece of land and grew corn and cotton and a little molasses cane. Some of it we used, and some of it Papa sold, but he really didn't have enough land to make much money, and by the time he got through paying the people he rented the land from and buying things from their store to farm with, he hardly had any money left.

I guess most of the time I was growing up, Papa worked at the train station, taking luggage off one train and putting it on another, and unloading crates of fruit, things like that. He worried a lot about not being able to buy us things. I remember one time Mama bought some

65

new shoes for my sister Roland. Mama had gone to a bigger town to get them because the store in Parmele had clothes that were so old-fashioned it wasn't funny.

Anyway, Mama bought Roland these pretty pumps. They were dark brown and had a square throat, and they were really pretty. When Mama got home, Papa said, "Why didn't you get some shoes for Lessie, too?" Mama told him she didn't have enough money, she'd have to save for a while, then it would be my turn.

But Papa wasn't satisfied. He went to the store in Parmele, and he came home and he said, "Daughter, Papa bought you some new shoes, too." I was so happy—until I saw the shoes. They were so ugly. They were real light tan, and nobody had worn any shoes that color in I don't know when! And they were turned up at the toe, kind of like an elf's shoes. But I said, "Thank you, Papa, thank you very much." Then I went off and cried and cried because those were just about the ugliest shoes I had ever seen.

66

Papa didn't get mad too often. Usually when I did something wrong, he would just say, "Now daughter, you know you shouldn't have done that," and I'd be so ashamed. But once in a while, he would get really mad. One time I talked back to Mama, and what did I do that for! Papa heard me and he yelled at me so loud it made my stomach hurt. He said, "What did you say!" I told him what I'd said, but he kept on asking me. And my answer kept getting softer and softer. Finally Papa said, "Your mama borned you into this world! Don't you ever talk to her like that again!" I said, "Yes, sir."

Another time he got mad was when he came home and there was a white man there selling insurance. We were sitting in the hall, all of us children and Mama, while this man tried to talk her into buying some insurance. Papa came home and he said, "My wife doesn't want any insurance, she doesn't want to buy anything!" The man got his hat and left in a hurry. Then Papa said, "He wouldn't want me to come to his front door, he wouldn't want me to talk to his wife. I don't want him in my house, and I don't want him to talk to my wife."

Papa could really get mad sometimes. But mostly, he was a quiet man. He gave us a lot of love.

"Jumpin' Sally"

"Here comes Jumpin' Sally, just a-running, plaits a-flying, high forehead a-shining." That's what my aunt, Sis Ada, used to say whenever she saw me coming. I was such a fidgety child. Unless I was reading or day-dreaming, I was hardly ever still. I was always singing to the top of my voice, or jumping rope, or running so fast I thought my feet weren't touching the ground, or drawing pictures in the dirt with a long stick, or playing dolls and paper dolls and mothers and school, hide-and-go-seek and hopscotch, and most of all, jacks.

We called them bobjacks, and we didn't use a rubber ball and little metal pieces like the ones children use now. We'd find some smooth, medium-sized rocks and we'd use one for the ball and the rest for bobjacks. And we had to be really fast because we couldn't wait and let the rock bounce the way you can with a ball. We had to catch it before it hit the ground.

I could have played bobjacks all day long, but Mama wouldn't let me. She'd say, "Go do some work now. Go chop the weeds, or sweep the yard." And then she'd say those words I hated to hear—"An idle mind is the devil's workshop."

On school days I was supposed to come straight home. I couldn't stop and play the way I wanted to. But one day I forgot. My friends were playing baseball, and I meant to get in the game for just a few minutes, but after I started playing, going home never even crossed my mind. All of a sudden I looked up, and there was Mama coming up the road to get me.

Mama didn't fuss, she just said, "Didn't I tell you to come straight home?"

I said, "Yes, ma'am."

She turned and started home, and I followed her, and all the way down the road, until I got out of sight, I could feel my friends' eyes dancing all up and down my back.

After that, I went straight home every day—for a while.

Hunger

When we lived in Mount Herman, Papa got paid once a week, and he would always bring groceries home on payday. But sometimes by the end of the week there'd be almost nothing in the house to eat, and Mama would try and mix up something to keep us from getting too hungry. Once, all we had was a little flour and cornmeal and sugar and lard, and Mama mixed it up with some water and baking powder and baked it. It tasted so good. We called it flour cornbread cake and we drank Postum with it because Mama never let us drink coffee.

Some days I would get so hungry that it was hard for me to play. I'd try to play games, but that pulling inside my stomach made me feel so bad. I had heard grown-ups say, "I'm so hungry I can see biscuits walking on crutches," and I would keep saying silly things like that to make myself laugh and feel better. But soon I'd have to give up playing and go lie down, not on my bed, but on the kitchen floor or the dining-room floor with my head under a table or a chair. I don't know why, but I just seemed to feel better with my head under something.

I'd lie there and try to doze off to make the time pass faster, and after a while, there would be my papa with his arms full of food, and everything would be all right.

Mama

Mama taught us how to draw, my sisters and me. She taught us how to draw little things like boxes and houses and love knots, and she showed us how to make rag dolls, and even some funny-looking dolls out of corncobs. And Mama really knew how to tell a story. She could make it sound as if it had really happened. She would have us sitting in chairs around her, and she'd read to us and tell us stories and recite poems. Pretty poems. And sad poems, too, sometimes.

One poem was about a little girl who was sick and dying. She kept on saying to her mother, "Put my little shoes away, put my little shoes away." She knew she wouldn't need her shoes anymore. We heard that poem so many times, but it always seemed so real and so sad, the way Mama recited it.

Mama loved to read. Sometimes she would get so wrapped up in a book, she'd stay awake all night long, reading. One morning I came in the kitchen while Mama was cooking breakfast, and she was shaking her head and saying, *"Umph, umph, umph."* Then she said, "I'll follow you to the end of the world and die like a dog at your feet."

I didn't know what in the world Mama was talking about, so I said, "What you say, Mama?"

She said, "Oh, it's just something I read."

That night she told Papa about it. She said it was the most romantic thing. "I'll follow you to the end of the world and die like a dog at your feet."

Papa broke out with a great big laugh. He said, "It sounds like foolishness to me."

I liked being near Mama. When she cooked, I would sit in a chair right near the stove and put my feet up on the woodbox and just talk and talk about all the different things I had been doing all day. And I especially liked being near her whenever I was scared.

I was scared to death of thunderstorms. One house that we lived in had a little knothole in the wall, and every time the lightning would flash, it looked like it was coming right through that hole. And the thunder was so loud. Mama would say, "The Lord's doing His work now, so you all go somewhere and be quiet." My sisters might

73

go somewhere else, but not me. I would sit right there up under Mama until the storm was over.

One night the Ku Klux Klan burned a wooden cross on Sugar Hill, and that was one of my really scared times. I was playing on the porch when I saw the cross. I couldn't see the wood, all I could see was those yellow, quivering flames in the shape of a cross, and I ran. I ran in the house to find my mama. I wanted to crawl up in her lap, under her apron, but I sat on the floor as close to her as I could get. I felt safe there, close to Mama.

Mama worked as a cook and waitress at Stokes' Cafe, down near the Parmele train station. She had to be at work early in the morning to fix breakfast for the people who would be coming in or going out on the trains. Afternoons, Mama would come home, and around four or five o'clock she had to go back and work until all the passengers and trainmen from the different trains had eaten their supper and all the trains had gone.

Even when Mama had been reading all night, she

didn't have any trouble getting up early. And she made us get up, too, before she left for work. In the summer when school was out, we'd watch her out the window and as soon as she got to the corner, we'd get back in those beds and go to sleep. Even my sister Roland, who usually obeyed Mama.

When we finally did get up, we had to rush around to get our work done in time. We had to get breakfast, make beds, sweep floors. The whole house had to be clean. Roland had to comb Mabel's hair, and I had to comb Lillie Mae's, and everybody had better be dressed and tidy by the time Mama got home.

I used to visit Mama sometimes at the cafe and drink a soda pop or something. I had to use the side door. The front door was for whites only, and they sat down at little tables to be served. Blacks used the side door and had to sit at a counter where we could only get snacks.

Mama would always be glad to see me when I went to visit her. But one day her face looked strange, like it was going to break up in a lot of little pieces. She didn't smile when she saw me, and I knew something bad had happened.

All day long I wondered what was wrong with my mama, and when she got home, she told us. She said there was this man who came in the cafe every day and the minute he sat down at the table, he wanted to be served. He called Mama *woman,* but he pronounced it "umman." He'd say, "Umman! Bring me a cup of coffee!" "Umman! Bring me a piece of pie!"

Mama didn't want to say anything to the man that might make her lose her job. She had been holding it all in, and that's what had made her face look so strange.

One day, though, Mama got so upset she told the man, "Don't call me umman! If you don't know how to talk to me, I can't wait on you!"

He never called her that again, but he didn't call her Mrs. Jones, either. He called my mama Pattie.

Horses and Cows

I was scared to death of both of them—horses and cows. My cousin Willie told me, "Don't ever wear red. A cow will run you if you wear red, she'll run you."

I never wanted to wear anything red. Horses and cows and pigs, too, walked all over Parmele just like people. Some owners would let their animals wander around and graze on other people's property, wherever there were no fences to keep them out. They even grazed in the weeds and wild onions, and sometimes a cow's milk would taste bitter and oniony.

I was so glad when North Carolina passed the "no-fence law." It made it against the law to let animals trespass, whether there was a fence around the property or not, so people had to keep their animals on their own land. But until that time, I was one scared little girl.

I remember one day I wanted to go visit Ma, Papa's mama. I always had fun over there. Ma had a pedal organ. Aunt Rillie would play it for me and sing, and she'd let me "play" it, too. And Aunt Cilla lived there, and she used to say all kinds of funny things. She could make up funny rhymes right on the spot. One of them went like this:

> *Well, I'll go home as quick as I can,*
> *Sit down and sop out the frying pan.*

I still laugh when I think of that one.

Well, anyway, I asked Mama one day if I could go over to Ma's by myself, and she said she guessed I was big enough. But by the time I was ready to go, a long freight train had come in and was standing on the railroad track, and I couldn't get across. I waited and waited, and when the train finally pulled out, that's when I saw the cows grazing all along the road. I couldn't go to Ma's. I wanted to go so bad, but I couldn't go. I was too scared. I turned around and went back home.

I felt sorry for a cow once, though. I was playing by myself in my backyard and some men came out into our neighbor's yard where some cows lived, and they took a gun and shot one of them right in the middle of her head. The blood just gushed all out from her nose and she fell to her knees. I couldn't stand it. I ran crying and screaming into the house. I couldn't stand seeing that cow get hurt. But it didn't make me one bit less afraid of horses and cows.

Learning the Hard Way

Mama used to say, "You always have to learn things the hard way, don't you, Lessie?" And I guess she was right. A lot of things I did learn the hard way. One thing was about kerosene lamps.

We didn't have electricity in our house, we used

kerosene lamps for lighting. They had to be lighted with matches, and the flame was covered by a glass tube called a lamp chimney. We used to wash the lamp chimneys every day so our lights would be nice and bright, and some nights I would look at that hot, shiny glass and I'd think to myself, "I bet I can touch it so fast that I won't even feel it." I just knew I could do it.

So one night when nobody was looking, I got close to a chimney, and I stuck out my tongue real fast and touched it, and oh boy! Did it burn! But I didn't tell Mama a thing about it because I knew exactly what she would say.

Martha Ann Barnes Ridley

I don't remember Mama's father. He died when I was a baby. But I remember her mother, my grandmother, very well. When I think about it, I can still see Mama

Ridley walking to church with her wicker basket over her arm. She was the church mother, and every fourth Sunday she baked the bread that would be broken into crumbs for Communion. She'd bake it pretty and brown and wrap it in a white cloth napkin and put it in her basket.

Every Thursday she took her Bible and went to missionary meeting. She could read her Bible some, but not too well. She had learned to read after she grew up, and she still had a hard time with some of the words, but good reader or not, she didn't have any doubts about what was sin and what wasn't.

When it came to sin, Mama Ridley meant business. And we could always tell when she meant business, too. If she looked straight at us with no hint of a smile on her mouth, or even in her eyes, when she said, "Come here to me! Come here to me, I said!" we knew we'd better get there fast.

One time she caught us dancing in her backyard, and we thought she was going to give us a switching. But she didn't. She fussed instead. She said, "Who give you your feet? Who lets you breathe? Who lets you move? Can you do it by yourself?"

She didn't give us a chance to answer. She kept on going. "No! God give you your feet. *He* give you breath, and *He* lets you move. And you can't think of nothing else to do but that!" She went on and on and on so long, she fussed so long, we almost wished she had hit us and let us go.

Sometimes, though, Mama Ridley was kind of soft with us grandchildren. My cousin Willie and I were playing outside one day and we got mad and started saying mean things to each other. Mama Ridley heard us and she said, "Just let me find my switch." But she was smiling and kind of halfheartedly looking around for a switch.

Cousin Willie started running, and I ran right behind him around the corner of the house. Mama Ridley's house was set on wooden blocks, about two feet off the ground, and when Willie and I stooped down and looked under the house, we could see Mama Ridley on the other side, coming after us. We could see her long gray dress swinging and her low-heeled black shoes, laced up and high-topped, as she lifted first one foot and then the other. We jumped up and ran some more, and looked again, and ran some more, but she caught on to our game and went back in the other direction. We ran right into her, and all three of us had a good laugh.

We knew when to play with Mama Ridley, all right. But we knew when she meant business, too.

Separation

I was about eight, I guess, when Mama left home. We were still living in Mount Herman then, and she and Papa weren't getting along very well. I didn't know what was wrong, but I knew they weren't getting along.

Mama got us together one day, all of us children, and talked to us. She said she had to leave. She said not to tell Papa, but that she was going back to Parmele to live with Mama Ridley. She was waiting for Mama Ridley to send her a letter with the train fare in it. Mama was going to take Lillie Mae with her, since she was still a baby, and Papa would take care of the rest of us. Our aunt, Sis Ada, who lived nearby, would help him.

We were hoping that that letter would never come, but one morning it did, and while Papa was at work, Mama got ready to go. All the time she was getting ready, she talked to us about being nice and keeping ourselves looking nice, and things like that. Then she kissed us good-bye and started to cry, and we cried and hugged her and kissed her back and kissed our baby sister. And when Mama went out the door and we saw it close, we just cried and cried and cried.

In a little while, we got dressed in the clothes Mama

had laid out for us, and we went on to school. But it was just a sad day all day long, and when we came home, it was a quiet house that we came home to, a sad, lonesome house because Mama wasn't there. We tried to play Old Maid cards and dominoes, but after a while, we gave up and just waited for Papa.

Papa came home and he said, "Where's your mama and the baby? In the dining room?" He started toward the dining room, and we told him, "No, Mama's gone away." We told him about the letter she had left for him on the dining-room mantel. Papa turned back around— he never turned just his head when he looked around, he always turned his whole body—he turned around and he looked so shocked, I wanted to bawl.

Papa went to read his letter. When he came back, his eyes were sad, but he saw the way we were looking and he didn't let them stay that way long. He said, "Come on now, you little duckies, stop looking like things so bad. We going to be all right." He went to the icebox and saw the food Mama had fixed for dinner. "Great day in the morning," he said, "put some plates on the table. We going to be all right, we going to be all right."

Papa took good care of us. All of us had chores to do to help keep the house clean, and Papa and my sister Roland did the cooking. Roland wasn't much older than I was, but she was almost like a mother to us, not letting us get hurt and seeing that Sis Ada got our clothes to be washed and ironed. Whenever Papa had to go out, we stayed with Sis Ada. Summers we spent in Parmele with Mama.

I don't remember how long Mama and Papa stayed apart, about two years, I guess. Then they decided to go back together, so Mama got her own house in Parmele and Papa sent us to live with her while he stayed in Mount Herman and worked and sent us money.

Once in a while he would visit us, but he couldn't spare the train fare to come very often.

Finally he came home to stay, and I was some kind of happy because we were all together again.

Talking

Whenever I really wanted something that I couldn't have, or wanted to do something I couldn't do, I would go off by myself and daydream. Only, I didn't call it daydreaming, I called it "talking." I didn't move my lips or say anything out loud. I was talking inside, although sometimes I did catch myself smiling.

"Talking" was my secret. I never told *anybody* about it before now. I used to "talk" sometimes while I was doing chores like sweeping the yard or helping Sis Ada iron our clothes, but most of the time I'd go off by myself and get still and quiet.

When Mama was away that time she left home, I "talked" a lot. When I did that, Mama was right there with me. Telling me things. Telling me stories. Laughing. I could always bring her near, and Lillie Mae would be sitting on her lap, laughing at me. But then somebody would call me, Papa maybe, and everything would fade away.

OPPOSITE PAGE, clockwise from top left: *Weston Little, age five (1910); Parmele train station, 1940's; Pattie Ridley Jones and daughter Lillie Mae, Parmele, 1928; Lillie Draper, Parmele, 1924.* THIS PAGE, top: *Lessie Jones Little, Washington, D.C., 1929;* bottom: *Weston Little and Lessie Jones, Parmele, 1923.*

World War I

I was almost eleven in the spring of 1917 when the United States entered the war. I remember the young men leaving—Sandy Mayo, George Coburn, Noah Andrews, and all the others. And people sad and crying, going to the train station to see their sons and their fellas off to fight in the war. In some towns the Red Cross would be at the station, giving out cigarettes and cups of coffee, first to the white soldiers and then to the black soldiers, if anything was left.

Most of the men went to France, and Mr. Henry Andrews got killed there. It was a sad time. Even the songs were sad, like the one that went:

So long, my dear old mother, don't you cry,
So long, Mother, kiss your boy good-bye.

Spanish Flu

It was a terrible new disease, and it spread so fast. A lot of people had it, and some were dying, not just in Parmele, but all over America and in Europe, too. So many children were catching it that our school had to be closed down.

Mabel, Roland, Lillie Mae, and I all got Spanish flu. I was so sick. I couldn't eat, I was aching all over and sore, and I felt heavy, like a sack of something just lying there in the bed. And my head! My head hurt so bad.

Papa was still living in Mount Herman at that time, and Mama had to take care of us by herself. Then she came down with the flu, and her mother had to take care of all of us. Mama Ridley came over every day and brought us some thin soup, and fed each one of us, and finally we got better. Mama Ridley didn't catch the flu, but Pa Jones, Papa's father, got sick and died. And that's when Papa came home to stay, and when he hugged me,

I just cried and cried because we had all been so sick, and because Pa had died, and because I was so glad to see my papa.

Booker T. Washington

Booker T. Washington, the famous educator, came to Parmele once. I didn't get to see him, but I heard all about it. Everybody was so excited. Mr. Washington had his own railroad car hooked on to the end of a regular passenger train, and the train stopped for about fifteen minutes and he came out on the balcony of his car and made a speech.

The people who invited him had set up a lot of chairs at the place where the train would stop. They set poles in the ground, tall poles about fifteen or sixteen feet high, and dipped rags into tar and tied them to the tops of the poles. It was winter, a late winter evening, and when the rags were lighted, the tar burned slowly and gave off a good light. There was a big crowd. People came from everywhere. They came from all around to hear Booker T. Washington speak.

I wasn't there, but I heard so much about it, I feel as if I saw it.

School

Parmele had good schools. Parents sent their children from all over North Carolina and from other states, too, to come to our schools. Parmele Training School and Higgs Roanoke Seminary.

I started school in Mount Herman, where we were living when I was six, but after we moved back to Parmele, I went to Higgs. Higgs had about a hundred

93

and fifty students and three buildings. Two of the buildings were wooden and weather-grayed, and that's where we had the kitchen, the dining room, the chapel, and the dormitory for the boys from out of town. The girls' dormitory was on the top floor of the new brick building, and the classrooms were on the first floor. We were so proud of that building.

The new building had radiators instead of a potbellied stove. Papa used to keep the fire going in the basement furnace so the radiators would stay nice and hot. The school couldn't afford to pay him in money, but the music teacher, Miss Gussie Cobb, used to give Mabel and Roland and me music lessons to make up for it.

Outside Higgs' chapel there was a big bell, hanging on a tall wooden frame. Every morning, a little before nine, one of the boys would pull on the heavy rope that rang the bell, and all the students would get in line at the chapel door. Then Miss Gussie would start playing her march music on the piano inside, and we'd march in and sit on long benches, girls on one side, boys on the other.

First, we'd sing a song from the school songbook. Then somebody would read a chapter from the Bible, and somebody else would say a prayer. Then, before we marched out and went to our classes, we'd sing one more song. The singing was my favorite part. When I was little, I'd sing loud, *"Joy, joy, joy, in the presence of the King . . . ,"* and I just knew I could really sing. One time I saw my cousin Rosalie and her friend, Frances, look around at me and grin, and I thought it was because I sounded so good. But now I'm not so sure.

Our classrooms had desks with the seats built on to them. They were wide seats, two children sat at each desk. We didn't have ball-point pens back then. Each desk had an inkwell, a little jar of ink that was set down in a hole in the desk, and we had to keep dipping our pens into the ink so they would write.

The principal of Higgs was Professor Nathaniel Hargraves. Fess. We called him Fess behind his back. He was our principal and the pastor of our church and one of our teachers, too. He was a hard teacher. If you got eighty-five on your paper from Fess, you were really happy. It was like getting a hundred from any other teacher.

We studied black history every week out of a book by Carter G. Woodson, but we called it Negro history then. And we had to learn the names of all the forty-eight states and the name of every bone in the body. We had to be able to stand up and recite every single one of them. Anybody who didn't know the work had to stay after school. Fess would say, "You're going to stay here until you learn it!" Sometimes it would be eight or nine o'clock at night when he'd finally let a student go home. He had a strap, too, a wide strap named Betsy, for the boys when they didn't behave. He'd say, "All right, Betsy will get you." And Betsy would, too. But Fess knew a lot, and we learned a lot.

My last year at Higgs, I received a pin for having the best grades in the high school. It was a beautiful pin, fourteen-karat gold, made like an open book. Only two of us were seniors that year, 1924, and we had our

graduation with the eighth graders at Olive Branch
Baptist Church. I had on a white organdy dress that
Mama had gotten Miss Mamie Jenkins to make for me,
and white shoes and stockings.

That day was one of my hungry days, and later on,
Mama told me that while she was watching me make my
farewell speech, she was thinking, "My child hasn't had a
thing to eat today." But it was a happy day for me
anyway. I was just glad to be part of all the excitement
and happy that Mama had been able to get some time off
from work to come and see me graduate.

My Best Friend

Lillie Belle Draper was my best friend. We played
together every chance we got. When Mama would send
me to the store or to the post office, I'd go out of my way
to go past Lillie's house, and I'd stand at her gate and

call, "Hey *Lil*-lie!" And she'd answer, "Hey *Les*-sie!"
She'd come out to the gate and we'd talk and talk until I
knew I had better get going.

Lillie's married sister, Isabel, lived next door to me,
and when Lillie would come in the summer to spend the
day with her, I'd go over, and we'd sit on the bottom step
of Isabel's front porch with our bare feet on the ground.
We'd draw pictures in the dirt while we talked and rub
them out with our hands. Or we'd rake the cool, damp
dirt on top of our feet and pack it down tight, then slide
our feet out, leaving a little cave we called a frog house.
And all the time, we'd be just talking.

Sometimes we'd go walking down the railroad track.
I'd take my bucket with me so I could fill it with the
nuggets of coal that had fallen from passing trains, and
take them home to use in the stove. Lillie would help me,
but the bucket didn't always get filled because we
stopped so much to talk.

We'd sit on the silky gray rails and stretch our legs out

toward the weeds and tall grass and talk about things like books or boys. And we talked about music a lot. Both of us were crazy about the piano. We wished we could play like some of the people we'd seen.

We used to talk about Sunday School and heaven. They had told us in Sunday School that when we died, we would go to heaven and never, never, have to leave.

Lillie would say, "Lessie, I just can't understand 'never.'"

And I'd say, "Me neither, Lillie."

We couldn't understand "never." We could understand "a long time," or "a long, long time," or even "a long, long, long time." But *never? Not ever?* How could that be? We'd say, "Never, never, never, never," and keep saying it until we were almost out of breath, and then we'd laugh and say that we would never, never, understand never.

I thought everything Lillie did was pretty. The way she walked, swinging along, throwing one foot out a little more than the other, as if she were walking to a bouncy kind of music. The poems she wrote, poems about trees and other growing things, and birds. The way she sang, leaning her head back with a faraway look in her eyes, as if she were in love with the words and the music, and making the sounds come out so easily.

We built part of a city once, Lillie and I, and her sister Rosa and my sister Mabel. We built Mount Herman out of wood on a vacant lot near my backyard. The new building for Higgs School was going up then, and there were a lot of pieces of wood lying around that nobody wanted, blocks of wood in all kinds of shapes, squares, triangles, rectangles. We used them to build the part of Portsmouth, Virginia, that I had lived in when I was little.

Every day we worked on it. We built Glasgow Street, that long street with avenues running across it. We built stores and houses, my house on Douglas Avenue and my Aunt Ada's on Mount Vernon Avenue. And Mount

Herman Baptist Church and Mount Herman School. Sometimes something would fall over, but we'd stand it up again.

At night I would think about what we were going to build the next day. I'd think about the real Mount Herman and try to remember every little thing about it. Lillie had never seen it, but once she said to me, "Lessie, when I'm in bed at night, I think about Mount Herman and almost believe I live there." One night she even dreamed about it.

When we finished, we let the city stand for a few days, then we tore it down and took the wooden blocks home for our mothers to use in our cookstoves.

Lillie and I had our lives all planned out. We were going to be schoolteachers. I was going to be just like Miss Estee Riddick, stick a pencil in my hair and walk up and down the classroom aisles calling out spelling words to my students. I would pronounce each syllable of every word just the way Miss Estee did.

But first we were going to college. We were going to Hampton Institute and be roommates, and we would make ninety-five to a hundred in all of our subjects. We even knew what kind of clothes we would have. Lillie wanted to look girlish. She said she didn't like "grownish-looking" clothes. But I wanted to dress like the young women. I was going to have pleated skirts in all colors, and shirtwaists to match, jersey dresses with white piqué collars, high-topped shoes in black and brown. For sitting around in our room, studying, I would have a wide-sleeved kimono like the one I had seen in the National Bellas Hess catalog, pink crepe with green and white umbrellas scattered all over it.

We never did get to Hampton, but we sure had all our plans made. I was a few years older than Lillie was, but we didn't stop to worry about how we would manage to go to college at the same time. We were going to be roommates at Hampton Institute, and that was all there was to it. After all, we were best friends.

Doing the Laundry

Mama washed clothes once a week, and it was really a big washing. We helped her—Roland, Mabel, and I, and Lillie Mae, too, when she got big enough. We did the laundry in the backyard. There was a pump on the back porch for drinking water, but we washed with water from the well. We would draw buckets of water from the well and fill the three metal tubs that sat on a long bench. Then we'd fill the big iron pot and put small chips from the woodpile under it, and start a fire to make the water boil.

First Mama would scrub the white clothes on the washboard in a tub of soapy water. Then we'd wring them all out by hand and empty the water. Next, Mama would put washing powder and a little bit of lye in the boiling water, and we'd put the clothes in there, and keep adding wood chips to the fire so it wouldn't go out. We had a long strong stick that had gotten white on the end from being in the boiling water so much, and we'd punch the clothes down with it and stir them around so they'd all get really clean.

After the clothes got a good boiling, Mama would lift them out with the stick, a few at a time, and put them back in the first tub. We'd help her carry the tub back to the bench and put fresh water in it, and she'd scrub them on the washboard again. Then we'd wring them out again and rinse them in clear water in the second tub. Then we'd wring them out another time and rinse them in the third tub that had clear water with bluing in it. That was the last rinse, so we'd wring them all out for the fourth and last time, and hang them up on the clothesline. But that wasn't all. We had to go back and do all the same things to the colored clothes, except that we didn't boil them or they would have faded.

Even in the winter we did the laundry outdoors, on the side of the house where the wind couldn't hit us but the sun could. We pushed our coat sleeves up and washed those clothes, and we were so cold. Sometimes the clothes would get freezing stiff while we were hanging them up. But hot days were almost as bad as cold. I remember one hot summer day when it had rained the night before, and after we finished washing, we were so tired we just plopped down on the front porch in the shade to rest. And I was thirsty, so I went back through the hall to the back porch to get a drink of water, and what did I see but Mama's pretty, clean clothes lying in the mud. One of the clotheslines had broken.

I ran and told Mama, and she just stood there looking at the muddy clothes. She didn't make a sound, but the tears ran out of her eyes and down her face. She looked so tired. And then she said, "Well, we'll just have to wash every single piece over again." We washed them over and hung them on the fence until Papa could fix the clothesline.

Mama didn't like to waste anything. Every time we finished washing the clothes, we had to get buckets and dip the water out of the iron pot and use it to scrub the kitchen and the hall and both porches. Sometimes the floors were already clean, and I couldn't see why Mama made us do it. But she said we didn't want to let that "good old hot sudsy water" go to waste. I don't know why she said "we." Maybe she didn't want to waste the water, but I did.

Farm Work

I used to love to feed the chickens. We had a lot of them, and I'd get bread crumbs, or sometimes I'd mix up cornmeal and water so that it wasn't too wet, just kind of half dry, and I'd take it out into the yard and throw it, and the chickens would gather all around me, bobbing their heads up and down, pecking at the food.

I liked sweeping the yards, too. We made our own

brooms. We broke off bunches of long, thin branches from bushes in the woods and tied them together in three places. We'd leave the bottom untied so that it stood out like a gathered skirt.

Working in the fields was what I didn't like. Sometimes I worked on Papa's little farm, but mostly my friends and I worked for white farmers, for pay. In the spring of the year, when the cotton plants had grown up just a few inches, we'd chop the weeds down with a hoe. In early summer we'd dig white potatoes out of the ground and separate them, put the big ones in one pile, the small ones in another, and then we'd go down the rows, picking them up and putting them in buckets. Then we had to take those heavy buckets and pour the potatoes into barrels.

Later on in the summer we worked in tobacco. There were four kinds of workers—breakers, truckers, handers, and loopers. The breakers would go out in the fields and break off the big tobacco leaves and put them in low wooden trucks. The truckers drove the horses that pulled the trucks from the fields to the shelter. That's where I would be, at the shelter. I was a hander. I would take bunches of leaves, three to a bunch, off the truck as fast as I could and hand them to my looper so she could tie them to a long stick. We had to work really fast, and if we saw a storm coming up, we didn't even stop for our midday meal.

In the fall we picked cotton. We'd start in early September and work until school opened, and after we'd been in school for a few weeks, we had to stop and pick cotton again for a while. A lot of children had to do that. Our families needed the money. But the teachers seemed to understand, and they'd see that we caught up with the rest of the class when we went back.

There was nothing that I liked about working in the fields. I mean *nothing!* Working in tobacco, the scent made me sick. Chopping weeds out of the cotton, the sun was too hot. Picking up potatoes, the buckets were too heavy and the sun was too hot. Picking cotton, you had to hang a burlap sack on your shoulder to put the cotton in, and pull it down the row as you picked, and when the sack started getting heavy, the strap cut into your shoulder. And my back would hurt so much from stooping over that sometimes I'd get on my knees and crawl. And then my knees would get sore. And the sun! The sun was so hot!

Then too, some of the people we worked for were mean, or insulting. One day my friends and I were supposed to pick cotton, and the farmer came around with his horse and cart and took us out to the farm. But when we got there, he didn't have any sacks, so he said, "Y'all go down the road to Aunt Sarah's and borrow some sacks."

We didn't like it that he was calling a black woman "aunt" instead of "miss," and since Lillie's sister, Annie Lee, was the biggest one of us, she spoke up.

"Is she your aunt?" Annie Lee said.

The farmer said, "She might be," and he gave us a smart-alecky look.

Well, what did he say that for! We all got mad. Annie Lee turned around and walked on off, and we followed right behind her. We got back on that sandy road and walked all the way home.

No, I didn't like field work one bit. But I did a lot of it anyway because we needed the money. The school didn't furnish our books, so I'd take my money and buy books, and if I had a few dollars left over, I'd buy a piece of pretty material so Mama could make me a dress.

Clothes

Every Sunday morning Papa would go to our church and ring the steeple bell. Everybody in town could hear it. It sounded like it was calling, "Come to church, come to church, come to church," and we would know it was time to put on our Sunday clothes.

In summer we wore white organdy or voile dresses that Mama had made. Long socks and patent-leather shoes. Straw hats, sometimes sailors with pink or blue or white streamers, and sometimes bonnet-shaped. In winter, blue middy blouses and pleated skirts, or long-sleeved dresses with belts. Ribbed stockings and laced high-topped shoes that came halfway up the leg, and velvet hats.

When Mama dressed up, she wore her black-and-white plaid suit. It had a velvet collar and an ankle-length skirt. It was called a dog-ear suit—the bottom of the jacket had points that looked like a dog's ears. I used to look at that suit and think to myself, "When I grow up, I'm going to have one just like it." I didn't realize that by the time I grew up, dog-ear suits would be way out of style.

For everyday, Mama wore a long dress and an apron tied around her waist. The apron would be starched and ironed into folds like a fan. Women wore hobble skirts back then, too. The skirts were so narrow at the ankle that short, short steps had to be taken. Mama could hardly lift her foot high enough to come up the steps.

One year we were all surprised—high-topped shoes, all of a sudden, went out of style. At first, those low shoes really looked strange, but then all the girls started getting them, and my sisters and I, we wanted them, too. We begged Mama, and we begged Papa, and finally we got some. It was really kind of funny because I could remember a time when all I wanted in the world was a pair of high-topped shoes.

Parties

Our school parties were called socials. We had them in the chapel, in the evening, and they'd last until about ten o'clock. We weren't allowed to stay out late.

First we'd have a program, recite poems and have skits, play the piano, sing solos and duets, things like that. After the program, we ate and played bobbing apples and fishing, and having our fortunes told. But the best part was the grand march. The boys and girls would get in line, two by two, and march. We'd march right up to the corners of the room and make sharp turns, and change partners sometimes. It was a lot of fun. But it wasn't dancing.

We weren't supposed to dance. The church didn't allow it, and most of the people in our town were church people. But, at house parties, we used to sneak and dance anyway. Maybe it wasn't really sneaking because some of our parents were always in the next room, but they pretended they didn't know we were dancing. We'd do the fox trot, and the Big Apple, and the Charleston, and the waltz, and picking cherries. Picking cherries, we'd reach up with first one arm and then the other, as if we were pulling cherries off a tree.

Mr. Jesse Grimes would come to some of our parties and play the blues on his guitar. And some of our friends had phonographs, and we'd put on some good records. The phonographs weren't electric, they had to be wound up, and while we were dancing, they would start to run down, and the music would get slower and slower and lower and lower until somebody wound them up again.

One night we were having a good old time at a party, just dancing with our fellas, but what we didn't know was that one of the church deacons was peeping in the window, spying on us. That man went back to the church and told on us. He told the pastor and the other deacons and some of the members, and they said we had sinned and would have to apologize.

Well, my sister Roland said she wasn't sorry and she wasn't going to apologize to anybody, and she didn't, either. But me, at the next business meeting—it was a Saturday morning—I went walking up to the front of the church just like a little mouse. I walked up there and I said, "I beg your pardon," and the tears were running all down my face. But even while I was saying it, I knew I was going to dance again just as soon as I got a chance.

My Fella

"I ain't got nobody." That's what Weston Little was saying the first time I ever saw him. He wasn't singing the words of the song, he was just saying them. But he wasn't talking to me. He was showing off for Roland, pretending he didn't have any friends.

Weston had come from Bethel to visit his cousins next door, and he was standing over there on their porch, hollering "I ain't got nobody" to Roland. I was wishing it was me he wanted to talk to. I thought he was really cute. I was almost thirteen that year, and Weston looked to be about fourteen, and he had large eyes and heavy eyebrows. I didn't find out until later what a big tease he was.

The next year he moved to Parmele, and he was always teasing somebody. Once when I was working on a farm, he threw a worm on me, a tobacco worm. I was scared to death of worms, and I just screamed. I was so mad with Weston. But the madder I got, the more he laughed.

I was seventeen when he started paying any attention to me. I used to go to the post office to pick up the mail for Mama and Papa, and after I'd get part of the way home, Weston would catch up with me and walk me the rest of the way. Then one day he wrote me a letter asking me if I would be his girl, and I wrote back and said yes, he could be my fella.

❦

I'm a great-grandmother now, and Weston is still my fella. We got married in Robersonville, North Carolina, on October 17, 1926, and we've had a long, good life together. We have five children. Our first was a boy, Weston Wilbur Little like his daddy. Our second was a girl. My mama named her Eloise.

Eloise Glynn Little Greenfield

BORN IN PARMELE, NORTH CAROLINA,

May 17, 1929

LANDSCAPE

❧

FIVE MONTHS after Eloise Little was born, the system of producing and selling goods in the United States failed, and the Great Depression began. Banks, farms, and many other businesses had to close. Millions of people lost their jobs.

Since 1915, blacks had been leaving the Deep South in large numbers. They had moved to cities such as Philadelphia, New York, Chicago, and Washington, D. C., expecting to find better conditions. What they found were problems that were slightly different, but every bit as harsh as those they had left behind. And now, in 1929, the Great Depression had come to add to their problems, and to rack most of America.

I'm Born

They say Mrs. Rovenia Mayo delivered more than a hundred babies in and around Parmele. I was one of them.

Mama wasn't expecting me until the end of the month, but I fooled her—I was ready to see the world on the seventeenth of May. Daddy was downtown playing checkers in front of Mr. Slim Gordon's store, and Mama wanted to wait until he came home, but his mother told her, "That young'un ain't going to wait for nobody! I'm going to get Mrs. Mayo now!"

I was born at six o'clock that evening. My great-aunt Mary was there to welcome me, and both of my grandmothers, Williamann Little and Pattie Ridley Jones. My brother Wilbur was there, too, but he didn't think my arrival was anything to get excited about— Mrs. Mayo had helped him make his grand entrance just the year before.

When Daddy came home, I was all of half an hour old, and did I give him a surprise!

Daddy Makes a Way

When I was three months old, Daddy left home to make a way for us. He went North, as thousands of black people had done, during slavery and since. They went North looking for safety, for justice, for freedom, for work, looking for a good life. Often one member of a family would go ahead of the others to make a way—to find a job and a place to live. And that's what my father did.

In the spring of 1926, Daddy had graduated from high school, Parmele Training School. He had been offered a scholarship by Knoxville College in Tennessee, but he hadn't taken it. He and Mama had gotten married that fall, and now they had Wilbur and me to take care of. Mama had been teaching school since her graduation from Higgs, but she had decided to stop.

Nineteen twenty-nine was a bad time for Daddy to go away, but a worse time for him not to go. The Great Depression was about to begin, had already begun for many people. All over the United States, thousands of people were already jobless and homeless.

In Parmele, there were few permanent jobs. Some seasons of the year, Daddy could get farm work, harvesting potatoes and working in the tobacco fields.

Every year, from August to around Thanksgiving, he worked ten hours a day for twenty-five cents an hour at a tobacco warehouse in a nearby town, packing tobacco in huge barrels and loading them on the train for shipping. And he and his father were house movers. Whenever somebody wanted a house moved from one place to another, Daddy and Pa would jack it up and attach it to a windlass, the machine that the horse would turn to move the house. But it was only once in a while that they were called on to do that.

So, one morning in August 1929, Mama went with Daddy to the train station and tried to hold back her tears as the Atlantic Coast Line train pulled out, taking him toward Washington, D.C. Then she went home, sat in the porch swing, and cried.

In Washington, friends helped Daddy find a room for himself and his family to live in, and took him job hunting. He found a job as a dishwasher in a restaurant, and in a few weeks, he had saved enough money for our train fare.

Mama brought Wilbur and me to our new home on a Saturday night. Two days later, Daddy was out of a job. The restaurant manager had tricked him. He hadn't told Daddy that he was being hired just until the regular dishwasher came back from vacation.

Daddy's next job lasted only two months. Then, finally, he found one at a Peoples Drug Store, making deliveries on a bicycle and cleaning the store. So we were in Washington to stay. Daddy worked at the drugstore for several years, and whenever they put a new display in the window, he would bring home the material from the old one, and Mama would dye it and make dresses and slips for herself and for me.

First Days

It's the first day of my life—my remembered life. I'm three years old, sitting on the floor with Mama. Cutting out a picture for my scrapbook, a picture of a loaf of bread. Cutting it out and pasting it in my book with the flour-and-water paste I had helped to make.

As far as I know, that was the day my life began.

My school life began two years later. Mama walked my cousin Vilma and me down P Street, through the open doors of John F. Cook School, and into Mrs. Staley's kindergarten class. Vilma and I were both scared. I was scared quiet; she was scared loud. I sat squeezed up in my chair, and Vilma screamed.

A Play

When I was in the fifth grade, I was famous for a whole day, and all because of a play. The teacher had given me a big part, and I didn't want it. I liked to be in plays where I could be part of a group, like being one of the talking trees, or dancing, or singing in the glee club. But having to talk by myself—*uh uh!*

I used to slide down in my chair and stare at my desk while the teacher was giving out the parts, so she wouldn't pay any attention to me, but this time it didn't work. She called on me anyway. I told her I didn't want to do it, but she said I had to. I guess she thought it would be good for me.

On the day of the play, I didn't make any mistakes. I remembered all of my lines. Only—nobody in the audience heard me. I couldn't make my voice come out loud.

For the rest of the day, I was famous. Children passing by my classroom door, children on the playground at lunchtime, kept pointing at me saying, "That's that girl! That's the one who didn't talk loud enough!"

I felt so bad, I wanted to go home. But one good thing came out of it all. The teacher was so angry, so upset, she told me that as long as I was in that school, I'd never have another chance to ruin one of her plays. And that was such good news, I could stand being famous for a day.

Watergate

Long before there was a Watergate break-in, or even the Watergate Apartments, there was the Watergate outdoor theater down on the Potomac River. It was a theater without walls or ceiling, and the stage was a ship that was docked there at the edge of the river. The audience sat on folding chairs, or on the wide concrete steps that rose above the ship. Usually you could sit on the steps free, but when you couldn't, we'd stand on the bridge. My little brother Gerald had been born by that time, and we'd all go and stand on the bridge and look down.

You could see everything from up there. And when it got dark, the river looked pretty with the reflection of the lights snake-dancing in the water. You could hear everything up there, too. Before the program started, the voices of the people in the audience floated up into the air and away, instead of being squeezed together in a roar the way they would have been in an auditorium.

On the stage, there was mostly opera. Singers acting out other times and other places—the eighteenth century, the nineteenth century, Spain, Italy, France, Japan. There were bright-colored costumes, marching choruses of soldiers, romance and broken hearts, and dancing and fighting and dying.

I liked the dying parts best of all. A woman in a long, puffed-out skirt, looking weak but singing strong and high, would sing a little and die a little, sing a little more, die a little more. Then she would slowly lift her arm and put the back of her hand to her forehead, sing one last short, high note—*"Oh!"*—and collapse on the couch. Then her boyfriend would fall to his knees beside her, crying and singing with his friends about how much he loved her and couldn't bear to live without her.

Oh, Watergate could be sad. So, so sad.

Langston Terrace

I fell in love with Langston Terrace the very first time I saw it. Our family had been living in two rooms of a three-story house when Mama and Daddy saw the newspaper article telling of the plans to build it. It was going to be a low-rent housing project in northeast Washington, and it would be named in honor of John Mercer Langston, the famous black lawyer, educator, and congressman.

So many people needed housing and wanted to live there, many more than there would be room for. They were all filling out applications, hoping to be one of the 274 families chosen. My parents filled out one, too.

I didn't want to move. I knew our house was crowded—there were eleven of us, six adults and five children—but I didn't want to leave my friends, and I didn't want to go to a strange place and be the new person in a neighborhood and a school where most of the other children already knew each other. I was eight years old, and I had been to three schools. We had moved five times since we'd been in Washington, each time trying to get more space and a better place to live. But rent was high so we'd always lived in a house with relatives and friends, and shared the rent.

One of the people in our big household was Lillie, Daddy's cousin and Mama's best friend. She and her husband also applied for a place in the new project, and during the months that it was being built, Lillie and Mama would sometimes walk fifteen blocks just to stand and watch the workmen digging holes and laying bricks. They'd just stand there watching and wishing. And at home, that was all they could talk about. "When we get our new place . . ." "If we get our new place . . . "

Lillie got her good news first. I can still see her and Mama standing at the bottom of the hall steps, hugging and laughing and crying, happy for Lillie, then sitting on the steps, worrying and wishing again for Mama.

135

Finally, one evening, a woman came to the house with our good news, and Mama and Daddy went over and picked out the house they wanted. We moved on my ninth birthday. Wilbur, Gerald, and I went to school that morning from one house, and when Daddy came to pick us up, he took us home to another one. All the furniture had been moved while we were in school.

Langston Terrace was a lovely birthday present. It was built on a hill, a group of tan brick houses and apartments with a playground as its center. The red mud surrounding the concrete walks had not yet been covered with black soil and grass seed, and the holes that would soon be homes for young trees were filled with rainwater. But it still looked beautiful to me.

We had a whole house all to ourselves. Upstairs and downstairs. Two bedrooms, and the living room would be my bedroom at night. Best of all, I wasn't the only new person. Everybody was new to this new little community, and by the time school opened in the fall, we had gotten used to each other and had made friends with other children in the neighborhood, too.

I guess most of the parents thought of the new place as an in-between place. They were glad to be there, but their dream was to save enough money to pay for a house that would be their own. Saving was hard, though, and slow, because each time somebody in a family got a raise on the job, it had to be reported to the manager of the project so that the rent could be raised, too. Most people stayed years longer than they had planned to, but they didn't let that stop them from enjoying life.

They formed a resident council to look into any neighborhood problems that might come up. They started a choral group and presented music and poetry programs on Sunday evenings in the social room or on the playground. On weekends, they played horseshoes and softball and other games. They had a reading club that met once a week at the Langston branch of the public library, after it opened in the basement of one of the apartment buildings.

The library was very close to my house. I could leave

by my back door and be there in two minutes. The playground was right in front of my house, and after my sister Vedie was born and we moved a few doors down to a three-bedroom house, I could just look out of my bedroom window to see if any of my friends were out playing.

There were so many games to play and things to do. We played hide-and-seek at the lamppost, paddle tennis and shuffleboard, dodge ball and jacks. We danced in fireplug showers, jumped rope to rhymes, played "Bouncy, Bouncy, Bally," swinging one leg over a bouncing ball, played baseball on a nearby field, had parties in the social room and bus trips to the beach. In the playroom, we played Ping-Pong and pool, learned to sew and embroider and crochet.

For us, Langston Terrace wasn't an in-between place. It was a growing-up place, a good growing-up place. Neighbors who cared, family and friends, and a lot of fun. Life was good. Not perfect, but good. We knew about problems, heard about them, saw them, lived through some hard ones ourselves, but our community wrapped itself around us, put itself between us and the hard knocks, to cushion the blows.

It's been many years since I moved away, but every once in a long while I go back, just to look at things and remember. The large stone animals that decorated the playground are still there. A walrus, a hippo, a frog, and two horses. They've started to crack now, but I remember when they first came to live with us. They were friends, to climb on or to lean against, or to gather around in the evening. You could sit on the frog's head and look way out over the city at the tall trees and rooftops.

Nowadays, whenever I run into old friends, mostly at a funeral, or maybe a wedding, after we've talked about how we've been and what we've been doing, and how old our children are, we always end up talking about our childtime in our old neighborhood. And somebody will say, "One of these days we ought to have a Langston

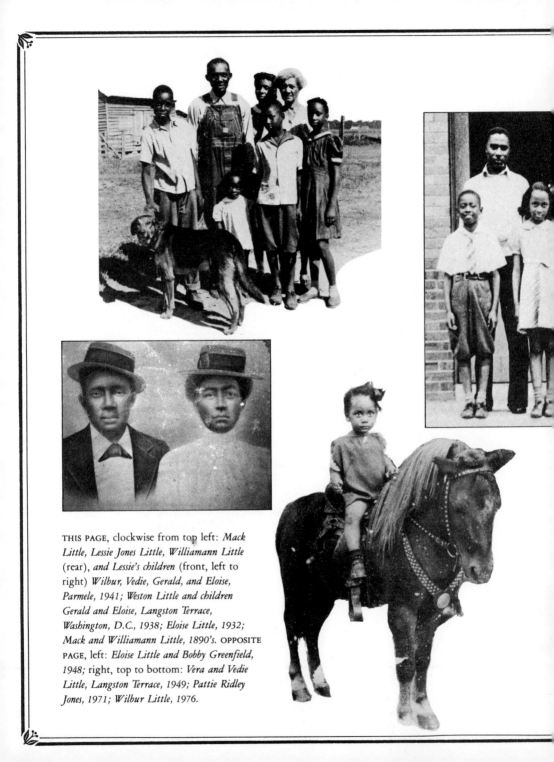

THIS PAGE, clockwise from top left: *Mack Little, Lessie Jones Little, Williamann Little* (rear), *and Lessie's children* (front, left to right) *Wilbur, Vedie, Gerald, and Eloise, Parmele, 1941; Weston Little and children Gerald and Eloise, Langston Terrace, Washington, D.C., 1938; Eloise Little, 1932; Mack and Williamann Little, 1890's.* OPPOSITE PAGE, left: *Eloise Little and Bobby Greenfield, 1948;* right, top to bottom: *Vera and Vedie Little, Langston Terrace, 1949; Pattie Ridley Jones, 1971; Wilbur Little, 1976.*

reunion." That's what we always called it, just "Langston," without the "Terrace." I guess because it sounded more homey. And that's what Langston was. It was home.

Mama Sewing

I don't know why Mama ever sewed for me. She sewed for other people, made beautiful dresses and suits and blouses, and got paid for doing it. But I don't know why she sewed for me. I was so mean.

It was all right in the days when she had to make my dresses a little longer in the front than in the back to make up for the way I stood, with my legs pushed back and my stomach stuck out. I was little then, and I trusted Mama. But when I got older, I worried.

Mama would turn the dress on the wrong side and slide it over my head, being careful not to let the pins stick me. She'd kneel on the floor with her pin cushion, fitting the dress on me, and I'd look down at that dress, at that lopsided, raw-edged, half-basted, half-pinned *thing*—and know that it was never going to look like anything. So I'd pout while Mama frowned and sighed and kept on pinning.

Sometimes she would sew all night, and in the morning I'd have a perfectly beautiful dress, just right for the school program or the party. I'd put it on, and I'd be so ashamed of the way I had acted. I'd be too ashamed to say I was sorry.

But Mama knew.

Joe Louis

Joe Louis was the heavyweight boxing champion of the world. They called him the Brown Bomber, and black people loved him. There wasn't any television in those days, but there was radio, and when Joe Louis fought, every radio in Langston was playing loud and clear.

We used to almost hold our breath, waiting to see what would happen, bite our lips and clench our fists to help Joe Louis win. And when he did, when the referee counted " . . . seven—eight—nine—ten!" people jumped up and yelled, phones rang, doors opened and friends who couldn't afford telephones came out on their porches to talk to each other about Joe Louis' victory, and theirs.

I remember a day when Joe Louis came to play golf on the nearby golf course, and that was all you could hear. "Joe Louis is on the golf course! Joe Louis is on the golf course!" Everybody rushed down there, children and adults.

A big crowd gathered to watch him play, and afterward our friends who had caddied told us every word he'd said while he was playing, and about the ice cream he had eaten at the clubhouse, and how they had stood right beside him and shaken his hand.

It was a big day, and we wouldn't stop talking about it for a long, long time.

Washington, D.C.

The Washington, D.C., I lived in didn't seem to have much to do with the place where the White House was located. I knew it was the same city, of course. Mama and Daddy had shown me that big white building on Pennsylvania Avenue, and when we lived on Fourth Street, President Franklin Roosevelt used to pass my house in the spring, sitting in the back of his long black car, lifting his hand to the people who had come outside to watch him on his way to Griffith Stadium to throw out the first baseball of the season. But I didn't feel as if I lived in the same city he lived in. I lived in a different place, a different Washington. . . .

❦

"*Ice*man! *Ice*man!" The iceman wouldn't let us miss him. Driving his horse and wagon, or his truck, up and down the streets, he would singsong so loud that people inside their houses would hear him and come out to buy big blocks of ice to put in their iceboxes and keep their food cold.

Other vendors, too, rode through the streets of my city, calling out their wares. "Apples! Get your apples here!" "Fresh fish!" "Tomatoes! Red, ripe tomatoes!" "Chickens here!" The chickens were live, in crates, and whoever bought them had to wring their necks to kill them, and put them in hot water to make the feather plucking easier.

When the photographer came around, he didn't yell. He knocked on doors, asking if children wanted to have their pictures taken sitting on his pony. And the organ grinder didn't yell, either. He stood on the corner, cranking the music out of the hand organ he carried. On his shoulder rode a monkey dressed up in a suit that had pockets, and when people threw money on the sidewalk, the monkey would jump down, pick it up, and pocket it.

The snowball man didn't have to yell. The children playing on the sidewalk did it for him. When they saw

146

him pushing his little white truck filled with crushed ice and syrups—lime, orange, cherry, strawberry, grape— they ran home in a chorus of yells. "Mama! The snowball man! Can I have a snowball?"

❁

"They dragging the river again."

Almost every summer of the years that I lived in Langston, I heard somebody say those words. Almost every summer, the police would drag nearby Kingman Lake—we called it a river—and bring up the body of a boy who had drowned. He would be a black boy, most likely from some part of northeast Washington. He would be a boy for whom fireplug showers were not enough. And because he wanted to swim, he would have died in the filthy water of Kingman Lake.

The boy could have gone to a pool and been watched over by lifeguards. Of course, he couldn't have gone to Rosedale pool, right down the street, or to most of the

147

pools in my city—they were for white children only. But if he had the streetcar fare, or if he felt like walking thirty or more blocks each way, he could have stood in a line three blocks long at one of the few black pools and hoped that enough children would get tired of the water and leave, so that he could take his turn before closing time.

But he hadn't wanted to do that. So he swam in the lake, and he died.

On the streetcars, we could sit anywhere, but we couldn't sit down at the drugstore soda fountains. We could shop downtown, but we might have to stand at the counter while the saleswoman waited on all the whites first, even if they had come in last, or we might not get waited on at all. The schools were segregated. The white newspapers carried only bits of news about black people, none of it good. The newspaper ads for all the best jobs said, "White Only." And if a "For Rent" sign in front of a house didn't say "Colored," black people could forget it.

There were a lot of things we couldn't do and places we couldn't go. Washington was a city for white people. But inside that city, there was another city. It didn't have a name and it wasn't all in one area, but it was where black people lived. There were black neighborhoods in different sections of the city, and black drugstores and schools in those neighborhoods. The *Washington Afro-American* and the *Pittsburgh Courier* newspapers were delivered there.

This city had a center. If you stood in the middle of U Street, N.W., and drew a wide, wide circle around you, you would be in the center of what was black Washington. Restaurants and hotels and Howard University and Miner Teachers College and nightclubs and Freedmen's Hospital and movies, and the Howard Theater where there were stage shows with music and chorus girls and comedy, and, once in a while, a play.

As with all places, there were both good and bad things about our city within a city. We had all the problems that the other Washington had, plus the problems caused by racism. Some people tried to drink their problems away. Some took their anger at racism out on each other. But most did what they could to help their friends and neighbors and relatives, and many got together to work for black freedom. There was always, in my Washington, a sense of people trying to make things better.

Chores

I used to think I had too much work to do. I had to make my bed, sweep the kitchen floor, and take turns washing the dishes. On Saturdays I'd dust and dust-mop my room and the living room. Once in a while I'd get a nickel for going to the store for a neighbor, and I helped Mama now and then with the laundry. Washing machines didn't have spin driers then, and I had to take each piece of clothing out of the water and put it through the wringer so the rollers could squeeze the water out of it.

I used to think I had a lot of chores to do, but after Mama and Grandma told me what they did when they were children, mine didn't seem like anything.

Parmele

Every summer we took a trip down home. Down home was Parmele.

To get ready for our trip, Daddy would spend days working on our old car, putting it in shape to go on the road, and Mama would wash and iron all of our clothes. Then everything would be packed in the tan leather suitcase and the black cardboard suitcase, and we'd be ready to go.

Mama and Daddy would sit in the front with Vedie in Mama's lap, and Wilbur, Gerald, and I sat in the back with our legs on top of the suitcases. This was before cars had trunks. Or radios. Or air conditioners or heaters. And there were no superhighways. The speed limit was forty-five miles an hour, and we went thirty-five to keep from straining the car.

It was an eight-hour trip to Norfolk, Virginia, where we always went first. Grandma Pattie Ridley Jones and Grandpa had moved there by that time, and we'd spend about a week with them, then go on to Parmele for another week.

On the road, I played peek-a-boo with Vedie between her naps. Or my brothers and I would count all the cars on the road. We'd say, "There go one! That's twenty-two. There go another one!" And we'd read out loud the rhymes on the red signs advertising Burma shaving cream, and wave at people sitting on their porches, and argue with each other until one of us got real mad and real loud and Mama told us we were giving her the jimjams and to be quiet.

One thing that we saw on the road frightened me.

Chain gangs. We saw them often, the lines of black men in their black-and-white-striped jail suits, chained by their ankles and watched over, as they repaired the roads, by white men with guns.

I wasn't afraid of the men, and I didn't think about maybe getting shot. But for a reason I didn't understand, I was afraid of the whole thing. Those bent-over striped backs, the sharp points of the picks the men swung, the sound of the picks hitting the concrete, the sight of men with long guns, pacing. It scared me.

After a few miles, that scared feeling would fade away, and I'd start to have fun again, or I might take a nap, and it always seemed as if days had passed before we finally crossed the line into Parmele.

By the time of my visits there, only a few trains were still passing through. My Parmele wasn't a train town or a mill town. It was a quiet town. Chinaberry trees and pump water and tree swings and figs and fat, pulpy grapes on the vine. People saying "hey" instead of "hi," the way they did in Washington, *hey-ey,* sending their

153

voices up, then down, softly, singing it through their noses. Parmele was me running from the chickens when I was little, riding around the yard in a goat-pulled cart, sitting on the porch and letting people going by in their cars wave at me, reading in the rocking chair, taking long walks to the gas station for soda pop with the children of Mama's and Daddy's childtime friends. Parmele was uncles and aunts and cousins. And Granny. And Pa.

They were Daddy's parents, Mack and Williamann Little. Black people in Parmele called them Mr. Mack and Miss Williamann. White people called them Uncle Mack and Ain' Williamann.

Granny was thin and whitehaired. She kept snuff tucked inside her bottom lip and wore aprons over her long dresses. I remember her most bending over the collards in her garden or feeding the chickens. She used to sew leftover material from my dresses into her patchwork quilts. She used to make apple jelly and green

tomato pickles. Anything her grandchildren wanted, she
wanted them to have.

And so did Pa.

Pa

"Leave the children alone," he used to tell mamas and
daddies. "They ain't doing nothing."

Pa was a sharecropper. He worked in the fields,
farming the land for the white man who owned it, and
got paid in a share of the crops he raised. Along with
that, he had almost always had some kind of little
business going, even when Daddy was a boy—a meat
market, an icehouse, a cleaner's, a grocery store.

Long before I was born, Pa had been a member of the
Marcus Garvey group that used to meet in Parmele on
Sunday afternoons. It was one of thousands of branches of
the United Negro Improvement Association headed by

155

Marcus Garvey. They met to talk about the beauty and strength of blackness, and to plan the return of black people to Africa.

I didn't think my grandfather was afraid of anything except the frogs that came out of the mud-filled ditches at night and flopped across the yard, and he knew plenty of names to call them. The thumb on his right hand looked like a little baldheaded man. The top joint had been cut off in a farm accident, and he had put it in a jar of preserving liquid that stayed on the front-room mantel. I never got tired of looking at it.

Children hung around Pa, nieces and nephews and neighbors, listening to his stories, giggling at his jokes. Some nights there would be just us—Wilbur, Gerald, and me, with our grandfather—sitting on the porch where the only light was that of the stars and the nearest house was a long way down the road. He'd tell scary stories, and get really tickled when we got scared. He swore his ghost stories were true.

"One night," he'd say, "me and my brother John was

coming 'cross that field over yonder." He'd make his arm tremble and point toward the woods across the highway. "And we commence to hearing this strange sound. Ummmmm-*umph!* Ummmmm-*umph!* And we looked up and saw this . . . this *haint!*"

He'd twist his face and narrow his eyes in horror as he stared out into the darkness, and I could just feel all those haints hovering behind us, daring us to turn around and run for the door.

Sometimes Pa would stop right in the middle of a story.

"Then what happened, Pa?" one of us would ask.

"Oh, I left after that," he'd say, and he'd laugh. Then we'd laugh, small nervous laughs, wanting to believe that it had all been just a joke.

Every year when it was time for us to leave, a sudden change would come over Pa. One minute he'd be challenging Daddy to a foot race that never took place, and the next minute he was weak and sick, trying to get us to stay. He didn't think he would live to see us the following summer, he'd say. At breakfast he'd begin the blessing with, "Lord, I sure do thank You for allowing me to see my family one last time before You call me home," and he'd pray a long, sad prayer that brought tears to our eyes.

But finally, when nothing worked, Pa would give up and help Daddy load the car with suitcases and with sacks of fresh corn and peanuts. There'd be hugs and kisses and more tears, and then we'd drive away, leaving him and Granny standing on the side of the road, waving, waving, waving, getting smaller and smaller, until they blended into one and disappeared.

Pa never liked to leave home. Granny came to visit us a few times over the years, but Pa always made an excuse. He couldn't get away right then, he had too much work to do, or something. One year, though, he had to come. He'd had a stroke, and Mama and Daddy brought him to Washington to take care of him. The stroke had damaged his body and his mind, so that he didn't understand much of what was going on around him, but he knew he

158

wasn't where he wanted to be. Mama would take him for a walk and he'd ask people on the street, "Which way is Parmele?"

My grandfather never got back to Parmele. He lived in Washington for eighteen months, and then, in 1951, at the age of seventy-eight, he died.

William and Pattie Ridley Jones

Grandma and Grandpa lived in Norfolk, Virginia. We visited them every summer, and whenever Grandma and her sisters and Mama and her sisters all got together at one house, there was a whole lot of talking going on, laughing and talking about things that had happened and people they had known when they were growing up in Parmele. And Aunt Mag, too, Grandpa's sister, would talk up a comical storm.

Grandpa was the quiet one. Every morning he'd ride his bicycle to his job as janitor in an apartment building for whites, and in the evening he'd sit out on the front porch and read the newspaper from front to back. Or he'd sit in the porch swing and sing or hum. It was a low, strong, beautiful sound when I was small. But I don't think I heard him sing after he got much older. He began to lose his hearing, and he lost most of his sight, too. But he continued to read the paper, even when he could see only one or two letters at a time.

In Norfolk, Grandma and Grandpa belonged to Mount Zion Church of God, Holiness, and mealtimes at their house started differently from the ones I was used to at home. Instead of just saying, "God is great, God is good, and we thank him for this food," each one of us had to say a Bible verse before Grandpa blessed the table. Sometimes we'd argue over who was going to say "Jesus wept," because it was the shortest verse in the Bible, and sometimes we'd run and get the Bible and memorize a new verse just before time to eat.

We loved eating Grandma's rolls, and her corn bread, too. But Grandpa didn't like the kind of corn bread we ate. Grandma made a special kind for him with nothing in it but cornmeal and water. Just cornmeal and water, mixed and browned in lard on a griddle on top of the stove. I didn't see how he could eat it, but he not only ate it, he enjoyed it.

Something happened to me one day in Norfolk that I won't ever forget. I was about twelve, and I was taking my first bus ride alone there. I can't remember where I was going, maybe to visit one of my cousins, but I remember what happened. The bus was crowded, so I got on and paid and stood next to the people who had gotten on in front of me, the way I would have done at home. But a drunk man sitting on the long side seat near the driver got very angry. He said, "You better get on back in the back where you belong!" I had forgotten that in Norfolk black people couldn't sit or stand in the front of the bus.

The people close by heard the man say it and they looked embarrassed, but they didn't say anything, so I squeezed through the crowd to get to the back, and then

I just stared out the window. I hated that drunk man and I hated those people for looking embarrassed. I felt as if everybody knew what had happened and I didn't know what look to put on my face. I was so glad when I got to my stop and I could get off the bus.

That was a terrible thing that happened, but it didn't ruin Norfolk for me. With so many relatives living there, every time we went, it was like a family reunion.

Martha Ann Barnes Ridley

I called my great-grandmother Mama Ridley, because that's what Mama called her. Actually, though, I don't think I ever really called her anything, except in my mind. I guess I must have talked to her sometimes, but I don't remember those times. I just remember that she was the small lady who lived in a bed, upstairs in Grandma's house.

Mama Ridley had fallen and broken her hip, and she never got out of bed again. She couldn't turn herself over, Grandpa had to do it, and she was in pain much of the time. But Mama told me that Mama Ridley loved her great-grandchildren. Whenever we got dressed up to go out, she'd say, "Let the children come in here before you go, so I can see what they got on." But nothing of her voice comes back to me. I can only see her lying there.

I was eight years old when Mama Ridley died. I wish so much that I had known her better. Hearing Mama and Grandma talk about her makes me know how much I missed.

World War II

In the beginning, I thought war was exciting. At twelve, I hadn't been paying much attention to all the news on the radio and in the movie newsreels about the fighting in

Europe, Africa, and Asia. Then, all of a sudden, the United States was at war with Japan. President Franklin D. Roosevelt came on the radio to say so. Mama and Daddy had known war before, and they were worried, but I wasn't.

The war changed our lives in a lot of ways. At school, they changed the way we saluted the flag so that it wouldn't look even slightly like the Nazi salute to Hitler, Germany's dictator. We sold savings stamps for ten cents apiece, or bought them and pasted them in little books, lending money to the government to help buy guns and ships and bullets. We learned new patriotic songs that we sang at all the assemblies. One song was written especially for black children to sing. We sang, "We Are Americans, Too."

At home, we watched the young men being drafted into the army. In a few weeks they'd come home on leave, looking older in their khaki uniforms than their friends who had been left behind and were still wearing pegged pants, ankle-tight at the bottom and baggy at the knee. Mothers were getting the jobs that had been held by men who were now soldiers, and their children had their own door keys dangling on chains around their necks.

We had air-raid drills, practicing for the time when an enemy plane might fly across the city looking for a place to drop its bombs. The sirens would blow and the air-raid wardens would come outside and patrol the streets, wearing hard white hats and armbands, and making sure that everybody else went inside and closed their heavy blackout window curtains if they had them, or turned off every single light. People sat talking in the dark, waiting for the all-clear sirens to sound.

Some things were rationed, which meant we couldn't buy them unless we had a special ticket to go with the money. Meat, sugar, butter, shoes, gas. Every few months the government gave out ration tickets, and when they were used up, we had to do without things until we got the next supply of tickets. Some summers

165

we couldn't get enough gas to take our vacation, but I didn't mind. It was for the soldiers and sailors and marines, so that they could have what they needed to fight the war.

War was exciting. Uniforms and blackouts and singing and sacrifice. There was always something going on. Something to talk about, something to think about, something to do.

And then, some of our Langston neighbors had to go to jail. They had joined a new group that we called "The Muslims." The men wore suits and ties every day, and the women wore long dresses and matching turban-style head wraps. We heard that they had meetings where they talked about a ship that was coming to take black people to freedom. When some of the men received orders to report to the army, they refused to go. They wouldn't go to the army. They had to go to jail.

And then, one night a woman received a telegram and screamed, screamed into the night and into my fading excitement. Her husband had been killed in the war.

War became real for me that night. I knew, then, what my parents had known all along.

High School

A few weeks before graduation from Browne Junior High School, all the graduates were given a sheet of paper to fill out. Written on that sheet of paper was the question we had been waiting three years for—what high school will you attend?

For days afterward, that was all we talked about. It meant we were really growing up. Leaving ninth grade, going on to high school. We went around asking each other, "What school did you pick, what school did you pick?" Finding out which of our friends would be going with us, and which we had to say good-bye to, as if we were losing them forever, as if all of the high schools were not within a few blocks of one another.

It was 1943, eleven years before the Supreme Court would order the desegregation of schools. There were three black high schools in Washington—Cardozo, Dunbar, and Armstrong. I chose Cardozo.

That building, the old Cardozo building, has been torn down now, but whenever I pass the place where it used to be, I think about news topics on Tuesdays, and passing friends in the corridors, and Coach Hall and the football team, and jumping up and down on the Brooks Stadium bleachers, and the girls' chorus, and homework, and falling in love.

And our principal, Mr. Mattingly, talking over the intercom, and pompadours and bangs, and jitterbugging in the gym, and dill pickles, and honey-dipped dough-nuts, and homework, and falling in love.

And favorite teachers and not-so-favorite teachers, and reindeer sweaters, and sloppy-joe sweaters a size too large with the sleeves pushed up. And homework. And falling in love. And looking forward to a graduation that would mean we were really, really growing up.

Black Music

My brother Wilbur plays the music called jazz, plays it on a stand-up bass in concert halls and nightclubs all over the world. Black music.

It has always been part of our lives. It's so much a part of me that if you could somehow subtract it from who I am, I would be a stranger to myself. I wouldn't know how to act. Spirituals, gospel, blues, rhythm-and-blues, jazz. Black music.

When I was a little girl, I used to hear Lillie singing, *"Some of these days, you're gonna miss me, honey,"* bluesing it around the house in her baby voice. At church, the choir would sing the gospel, or take a white hymn and bend it black. And the male quartet at Grandma's church would stomp and shout in harmony, looking hard at something in the air, straining the veins in their necks, until people here and there in the room got the Holy Ghost and did their shout-dances, even Grandma, a prim shouter, jumping up and down in one spot.

We sang spirituals in the glee club at school, and danced to black music on records, and I don't think we could have fallen in love if Billie Holiday hadn't sung "Lover Man" in that sad, lonely way.

I don't know how many hours, all together, I spent at the Howard Theater where the great musicians came to play. I could never see a show just once, I'd have to stay there and see it at least one more time. We called it "bucking the show." My cousin Vilma and I bucked the show three times one Saturday, went to the one o'clock afternoon show and didn't get home until ten that night. Mama was waiting at the bus stop, worried to death, when we got off the bus. We just couldn't leave that music.

At the Howard Theater, we could hear Eddie Mr. Cleanhead Vinson singing the blues, Coleman Hawkins mellow-horning on the tenor sax, Count Basie's band riffing the "One O'Clock Jump," Ella Fitzgerald scat-singing, playing her voice like a horn, Billy Eckstine, Savannah Churchill, Bullmoose Jackson . . . everybody came to perform for us at the Howard. And when Lionel Hampton came and sang out, *"Hey-bop-a-ree-bop!"* we sang it back. We sang that black music right back at him. *Black* music. You can still hear Africa in it.

Bobby Greenfield

In the spring of 1945, Bobby Greenfield was drafted into World War II. The night before he left, a bunch of us gathered around the stone horse in Langston and talked and joked with him about nothing important. It was our way of saying that we would miss him.

Bobby had moved into our neighborhood, right down the block from Langston, when I was thirteen. His friends told me he liked me. My friends told him I liked him. But the years passed, and we never told each other. The night before he left for the army, he promised to write.

The whole time Bobby was away, we wrote long, friendly letters to each other. Nobody reading them would have guessed that five years later we would be married.

A New Sister

It was not long after my high school graduation that Mama told me about the baby she was going to have. I had two brothers and one sister, and I wanted another sister, but I wasn't going to get excited about a little thing like a baby. I was too grown up for that, I was almost a full-grown woman.

I had been only ten when Vedie was born, too young to always think about acting unconcerned. Right after she was born that morning, I had heard her crying. Four o'clock in the morning, I was asleep on my sofa bed in the living room, and she was upstairs crying that new-baby kind of crying, *a-laaagh! a-laaagh! a-laaagh!* I woke right up. I kept my eyes closed, though, until I heard the doctor leave, and then I went upstairs to look at my baby sister.

But that had been a long time before. This time was going to be different. At least, that's what I thought. Then we started getting the house ready for the new baby, deciding where to put the crib, and buying clothes. And we had a long family meeting to pick out a name. For a girl, we chose Vera, and I can't remember the name we chose for a boy because we never had to use it.

I was almost eighteen when Vera was born, but that didn't stop me from running to the window and yelling to a friend, "Hey! I got a new sister!" I forgot I was almost a full-grown woman.

Family

Family. All this running through my mind. . . .

Saturday Sunday mornings Daddy making pancakes big as the plate Daddy making fat hamburgers leftover stuffed with rice green peas enough for everybody. Hot nights leave our hot one room sleep till midnight pillows blankets grass bed beside the river. Lincoln Park evenings Mama other mothers bench-talk children playing.

Give Mama her lesson take my piano lesson teach Mama. Downtown Wilbur Gerald Eloise wait in the car have fun get mad have fun get mad. Go for a ride park car New York Avenue hill dark watch trains wave passengers sitting in lighted window squares sliding by. Gerald tell us the movie tell us show us be the gangster be the good guy be the funny guy tell us show us. Look out the window wait wait snow stopping Daddy going to make snow ice cream ready to eat without freezing.

Vedie little sister turning somersaults we laugh. Vera baby sister fat baby laughing we laugh. Play games I'm thinking of a word I'm thinking of a word that starts with *S* guess give a clue it's blue. Radio hear-see squeaking door ghosts scary music. Parade take turns on Daddy's shoulder watch the floats watch the firemen march watch the horns watch the sound of the bass drum.

Easter Monday picnic zoo dyed eggs lionhouse popcorn polar bear picnic. Merry-go-round Mama laughing. Sparrow's Beach sun water-splashing sandy legs Mama laughing. Mama laughing. . . .

All this running through my mind now, running through my mind now.

Family.

Well—our stories are told. Grandma's, Mama's, and mine. It's been good, stopping for a while to catch up to the past. It has filled me with both a great sadness and a great joy. Sadness to look back at suffering, joy to feel the unbreakable threads of strength.

Now, it's time for us to look forward again, to see where it is that we're going. Maybe years from now, our descendants will want to stop and tell the story of their time and their place in this procession of children.

A childtime is a mighty thing.

EPILOGUE

Pattie Ridley Jones died in Washington, D.C., on June 16, 1972. She was eighty-seven years old. In her last years, encouraged by the publication of her granddaughter's stories, she began to write. Her long interest in books and words had developed into an interest in writing, and she wrote about her life. Though much of her section of this book has been drawn from the true stories that she had told us through the years and from interviews with family members, a good part of it was adapted from her manuscripts.

Because of our love for her,
because we are grateful that she gave us her love,
and because of the inspiration that her life was to us,
we hereby dedicate this book

TO THE MEMORY OF
PATTIE RIDLEY JONES,
OUR MOTHER AND GRANDMOTHER